THREE PLAYS

THREE PLAYS

MELISSA ARCTIC

ORANGE FLOWER WATER

THE PAVILION

Craig Wright

Foreword by Jane Hamilton

NORTHWESTERN UNIVERSITY PRESS
EVANSTON, ILLINOIS

Northwestern University Press
www.nupress.northwestern.edu

Printed in the United States of America
10 9 8 7 6 5 4 3 2 1

LIBRARY OF CONGRESS CATALOGING-IN-PUBLICATION DATA
Wright, Craig, 1965–
    [Plays. Selections]
    Three plays : Melissa Arctic, Orange flower water, and The pavilion / Craig Wright ; foreword by Jane Hamilton.
        p. cm.
    ISBN 978-0-8101-2814-9 (pbk. : alk. paper)
    1. Minnesota—Drama. I. Wright, Craig, 1965– Melissa Arctic. II. Wright, Craig, 1965– Orange flower water. III. Wright, Craig, 1965– Pavilion. IV. Title. V. Title: Melissa Arctic. VI. Title: Orange flower water. VII. Title: Pavilion.
PS3573.R5322A6 2012
812.54—dc23

                                                                                        2011043117

CONTENTS

FOREWORD

Jane Hamilton

It's natural to assume that any playwright loves the theater. But Craig Wright, he is *in* love! He's in love with the form of the play, he's in love with how people talk, he's in love with all the time-honored theatrical tools, the old magic, the playwright's sleeves stuffed with amazements. Out comes the deus ex machina, and there's the ghost of the Greek chorus (along with the update of Thornton Wilder's stage manager). He loves the flexibility of the form, and he honors the history of the art—the characters, for instance, stepping out to address the audience, Wright giving them the gift of the soliloquy. By using tableaux, he shows us how it is, right now, *right now,* freeze, time. His characters get to break into song, and the comic characters stumble in at the exact moment for relief. And why not bring to life that most famous of stage directions? *Exit, chased by a bear.* Lindy, in *Melissa Arctic,* peels across the stage, a bear on his tail. This is the stuff of joy.

There is, though, no self-consciousness, no coyness about the tricks, the tools, and yet Wright without flash in these plays calls our attention to where we are: you, he is saying, are at that most wonderful of places, the theater. We see his own relish in the form, an infectious happiness. You can't help but be hopeful, reading this collection. The stubborn old art will remain alive and well in the age of all the media we wring our hands over, those novel-reading, playgoing killers. With playwrights like Wright at work, the play must thrive.

In Wright's universe ordinary people are in usual circumstances, the basic stuff of life. You've got your marriage, your high school reunion. You've got your lunatic husband, the berserk guy who handily destroys what he should love best. Give Wright one couple, and he'll happily make a mess. Give him two couples, a bare stage save for a bed and end table, and those four actors will have a riotous time doing the work of fucking up pretty much everything. Off they go, to war.

In an essay Willa Cather wrote about Katherine Mansfield, she talks about the tension in every family, how "the mere struggle to have anything of one's own, to be one's self at all, creates an element of strain that keeps everybody almost at the breaking point." She describes the tension that could be said to animate Wright's work:

> Even in harmonious families there is this double life: the group life, which is the one we can observe in our neighbour's household, and, underneath, another—secret and passionate and intense—which is the real life that stamps the faces and gives character to the voices of our friends. Always in his mind each member of these social units is escaping, running away, trying to break the net which circumstances and his own affections have woven about him.[1]

Wright shows us his characters at the point where the interior, real life has broken through and compelled them to wreak havoc. There is the question that haunts his married couples: "Couldn't I have been happy with someone other than you?" Wright seems to answer, "Maybe yes, maybe no." What is more important, perhaps, than the fulfillment is the dream of that someone else, the rapturous memory or the radiant projection.

In a Wright play, the characters muck around in their own unhappiness until they get stopped in their tracks. Wright does his abracadabra to ennoble their suffering not by making it large and loud, but more often than not by making their humanness beautifully small—his helpless, poignant people alone together in the universe. Sometimes those helpless, poignant people, even at the point of violence, are blessed, as they say, with hysterically funny lines. And every now and again, Wright, who cannot be heartless for too long, allows his characters a transcendent moment. The ordinary circumstances are made fresh because he knows in what proportions to mix up the sublime and the mundane, lacing both with brutal humor or sweet humor.

Orange Flower Water has a seemingly simple setup: two couples, four chairs at the edge of the stage, the bed, and one regulation-size Beanie Baby. You want to know what would have happened if Hermia, Helena, Demetrius, and Lysander had been adults in Pine City, Minnesota, circa 2000? This is the play for you. The characters are distinct, to be sure, they are deeply themselves, and yet, as is true of the lovers in *A Midsummer Night's Dream,* they are also in many ways interchangeable. That is to say, they are programmed to screw it up. Near the beginning, David articulates the dream of all illicit lovers. Beth, in the motel room, asks, "So where are we?"

David: "We're in a bay in a kingdom in the clouds, and it's clear and it's quiet and it's beautiful . . . and *it's just us.*"

The truth is, of course, that it is never *just us.* It's our spouses and our children, and this thing we're doing will make war, because the institution of marriage invites war, and because by being in this motel room we've drawn the lines of the battlefield. In *Orange Flower Water,* it is Cathy who illuminates the sadness of the fallout. The scene in which she fights her way to David, her husband, fighting her way into lovemaking, the last time they'll have sex, is threaded through with equal parts anger and love, and a nearly unbearable sadness. In between the wars of the couples there is, naturally, the soccer field. This is, after all, parenting in America. The two men talk without saying outright what they mean while watching the game; the two women do the same but also they share a box of sour Skittles.

Wright's tenderness for children comes through in all the plays—the hope for the future that children always embody—but more interesting than that hope for Wright is the power of the parent's love, the knockout quality of that love, the way it changes the parent and informs him, the way it makes suffering worthwhile.

In *Melissa Arctic* Paul says, "All the other relationships come out of being a parent. You love your wife because you love your son; you love your husband because you love your daughter; you love what is because you love what might be." Wright seasons that piece of wisdom with Carl's response: "Not everyone feels that way."

If there is tenderness for children, there is tenderness, too, for the young lovers in *Melissa Arctic.* I have not read a dreamier, sweeter, but also bittersweet hypnotism scene—hypnotism, not to induce love but to charm the partner into fleeing into his own life, and then, the surprising turn of the second hypnotism, the charm for staying together, for committing, for heading hand in hand into the thicket of marriage.

Wright not only knows his characters deeply, but he respects the complexity of their feelings and the mystery of their personalities. Because he knows them so well, he can deliver them to the audience with great economy. Back to Cather, who said, "Art . . . should simplify. That, indeed, is very nearly the whole of the higher artistic process; finding what conventions of form and what detail one can do without and yet preserve the spirit of the whole—so that all that one has suppressed and cut away is there to the reader's consciousness as much as if it were in type on the page."[2] A good trick, if you can pull it off. And Wright can: there is no excess in these plays, and yet all the essential pieces are in place.

In *The Pavilion*, with three actors, voila: the buzzing room of the high school reunion. Oh, to be an actor, and to have the privilege of snagging the part of the narrator, the plummiest of the roles. Wright gives the narrator the work of setting the scene, starting with creation, and then taking us through the sweep of history.

> Monkeys in slow motion turn into women and men and soon campfires dot the plains for days in every direction . . . Christ is born, and a second later, nailed to a tree; Europe is invented and then the Renaissance and then the Enlightenment and then the steam engine and then suddenly!—*his family* came to Minnesota in the late 1800s. From Finland . . .

The narrator keeps zooming in, smaller, smaller, until we are in Pine City, on the shores of Lake Melissa. We're in the Pavilion at a high school reunion.

> PETER: Pudge?! Is that you?
> NARRATOR [*as* PUDGE]: It's me!
> PETER: You've lost weight!
> NARRATOR: You know what, I haven't! My body has changed, but I still weigh the same!
> PETER: You look great, though!

In two pages Wright creates the universe, he describes the flow of history, and he sets us down in a small Minnesota town. The spell has been cast even as we are laughing. The world has been made in order that Pine City might exist.

My guess is that Wright was as happy as a playwright could be, making *The Pavilion*. Men and women talking—talking about their lives, about their failures, about the essential characteristics of the sexes. Smoke, a man, says, "Men are born with a certain capacity for feeling—like women, they've only got so many eggs—men only have so many feelings." Kari offers a corrective to that stupidest of bromides from *Love Story* when she says, "Saying you're sorry doesn't change the position I've been put in! 'Sorry' isn't even a word! 'Sorry' is just a noise people make when nothing else can happen!"

The narrator runs the show, makes the magic, and reveals how the magic is made in the same breath. He says to the tech people, "Would it be asking too much to actually have the northern hemisphere near the summer solstice in the year 2005? Quickly?"

There's a thrill—because this is the theater! And anything can happen in the theater. When Kari says to Peter, "For you and me to start over, the entire universe would have to begin again," Peter can't help but ask the narrator, "Listen, can you start the entire universe all over again?"

The answer, sadly, is no.

It's hard to say how much of Wright's divided heart is given to straight-up romanticism and how much to cynicism, the comic's delight. His predilections spring up in varying doses in his characters, the plays themselves volleying for this position, that position. "Of course my heart's broken," Peter says at the end of *The Pavilion*, "but all in all I'm very happy because life's been good." It is that tension—the tension between sorrow and gratitude—that informs Wright's vision.

The pleasure of acting in these plays must be keen and deep. How wonderful to live in the characters and to say their lines. And how lucky are those of us who have seen Craig Wright's work. Once more to Cather: "The qualities of a second-rate writer can easily be defined, but a first-rate writer can only be experienced."[3] Here they are, the plays.

NOTES

1. Willa Cather, *Stories, Poems, and Other Writings* (New York: Penguin, 1992), 977–78.
2. Ibid., 939.
3. Ibid., 877.

THREE PLAYS

MELISSA ARCTIC

Based on Shakespeare's *The Winter's Tale*

PRODUCTION HISTORY

Melissa Arctic was commissioned by The Jungle Theater, Minneapolis, Minnesota, and originally produced by the Folger Shakespeare Library (Janet Alexander Griffin, artistic producer; Janet M. Clark, theater operations manager) in Washington, D.C., from January 23 to February 29, 2004. It was directed by Aaron Posner; the set design was by Tony Cisek; the lighting design was by Dan Covey; the costume design was by Kate Turner-Walker; the musical direction and sound design were by James Sugg; the properties design was by Shannon Thomas Kennedy; and the stage manager was Annica Grahamm. The cast was as follows:

Time	Kiah Victoria
Leonard Mattson	Ian Merrill Peakes
Mina Mattson	Holly Twyford
Paul Anderson	Kelly AuCoin
Melissa Willoughby	Miriam Liora Ganz
Carl Kuchenmeister	Kyle Thomas
Cindy Linda	Dori Legg
Alan "Lindy" Linda	Michael Willis
Mike Goebel	James Sugg
Musician	James Sugg
Alec Willoughby	David Marks
Ferris Anderson	Mark Jude Sullivan
Fisherman One	Michael Willis
Fisherman Two	James Sugg
Fisherman Three	Kiah Victoria

CHARACTERS

Time, *as Chorus (played by a young child)*
Leonard Mattson, *a barber*
Mina Mattson, *Leonard's wife, birth mother to Melissa*
Paul Anderson, *a recently divorced CEO of a prosperous clothing/woolens company*
Melissa Willoughby, *an adolescent*
Carl Kuchenmeister, *a deaf barber, business partner to Leonard*
Cindy Linda, *an artist and best friend to Mina*
Alan "Lindy" Linda, *husband to Cindy*
Mike Goebel, *a hospital chaplain (doubles Musician)*
Musician (*doubles Mike and Fisherman Two*)
Alec Willoughby, *a flower farmer, adoptive father to Melissa*
Ferris Anderson, *son of Paul, an adolescent*
Fisherman One/Two/Three (*played by the actors playing Mike, Lindy, and Time*)

SCENE

The play is set in Minnesota, in various locales in and around Pine City (in the north) and Farmington (in the south). Act 1 takes place in 1970, act 2 in 1988.

PERFORMANCE NOTES

The character of Time should appear momentarily or throughout every scene of the play, unnoticed (except for a few rare instances) by the other characters.

Every scene should begin with a tableau, like a painting, and then come to life.

Also, this play is one in a series of plays that includes *Molly's Delicious*, *The Pavilion*, *Orange Flower Water*, *Mistakes Were Made*, and *Grace*. They all take place in or involve characters from the mythical town of Pine City, Minnesota.

ACT 1

SCENE 1

[*Lights rise on* TIME. TIME *sings.*]

TIME: EVERYTHING BE STILL
EVERYTHING BE STILL
CAN EVERYTHING BE PERFECTLY STILL?

EVERYTHING BE STILL
EVERYTHING BE STILL
CAN EVERYTHING BE PERFECTLY STILL?

STOP THE CHANGING
STOP THE GROWING
STOP THE SHIFTING
STOP THE FLOWING
STOP THE GREENING
STOP THE LEAVING
STOP THE STARTING
AND DEPARTING
STOP THE BLOOMING
STOP THE BLOWING
STOP THE CONSTANT OVERFLOWING
AND LET EVERYTHING BE STILL
EVERYTHING BE STILL
CAN EVERYTHING BE PERFECTLY STILL?

[*The actors freeze in a tableau for scene 2.*]

TIME [*spoken*]: GO!

SCENE 2

[*Lights rise on a room in* LEONARD *and* MINA'S *home, where* LEONARD *and* PAUL *are watching TV.* LEONARD *is holding* MELISSA, *a baby.*]

PAUL: I'm leaving tomorrow.
LEONARD: Bullshit. Who am I gonna go ice fishing with if you go home?
PAUL: Isn't Carl missing you a little down at the barbershop? A little?

LEONARD: Thanks to Pastor Ed and his heavenly new shopping mall, Carl and the two customers a day are getting along just fine.

MINA [*from offstage*]: Who wants sloppy joes?

PAUL: Me!

LEONARD: Me. [*To* PAUL] Come on, stay. Don't be an asshole.

PAUL: I've been here two and a half weeks, Lenny. I have to go home.

LEONARD: No, you don't, you're a magnate. You're a man of substance. You don't have to do anything you don't want to do.

PAUL: That call I got last night, you know what that was? Two of the looms at the plant are down. And a third one is still waiting for parts—

LEONARD: They'll figure it out.

PAUL: I wish that were true.

LEONARD: I mean, what's so complicated? It's a loom!

PAUL: It's not the loom that's complicated; it's the people!

MINA [*from offstage*]: Fritos?

PAUL: Me!

LEONARD: Me. [*To* PAUL] I'll make you a deal. If the Vikes win, you stay.

PAUL: They won't win.

LEONARD: Fifty bucks.

PAUL: Why do you always do this?

LEONARD: You've got the money.

PAUL: Yeah, but—do you?

LEONARD: Twenty-five bucks!

PAUL: Ten bucks!

LEONARD: Twenty bucks!

PAUL: Twenty bucks. But I'm going tomorrow. I am.

LEONARD: Do you remember what it's like to be married?

PAUL: Lenny! You're the luckiest guy in the world.

LEONARD: I know, I know!

PAUL: I can't stay here to make your marriage work.

LEONARD: I'm not asking you to stay to make my marriage work.

PAUL: I have a son.

LEONARD: And I have a daughter. Have him come up. It's not like you're doing time.

PAUL: No, but—

LEONARD: You like ice fishing.

PAUL: I do like ice fishing.

LEONARD: You like drinking.

PAUL: I like drinking.

MINA [*from offstage*]: Beer?

PAUL: I'm good!

LEONARD: Me! [*To* PAUL] You should've gotten divorced a lot sooner.

PAUL: I never should've gotten married in the first place.

LEONARD: What we shoulda done is we shoulda bought that land out past Johnson's Bees like we said we were gonna, put a couple houses on it, and when you were damn good and ready, you coulda married Kjersty Linda.

PAUL: Kjersty Linda never woulda had me.

LEONARD: Where is she now, anyway?

PAUL: Who?

LEONARD: The Creature from the Black Lagoon.

PAUL: The mother of my child is in Saskatchewan.

LEONARD: You're kidding me.

PAUL: No.

LEONARD [*making a joke, rhyming with "vagina"*]: In Regina?

PAUL: No.

LEONARD: I thought she might be way up in Regina.

PAUL: She's out by Saskatoon. He's got a hunting lodge and a whole little luxury compound up there, it's sick. She turns her back on her son and she gets this storybook happy ending—it's so sick!

LEONARD: You ever wanna go up there?

PAUL: Why would I want to go up there?

LEONARD: No, I mean, deep up in there. Canada. The Yukon. The white emptiness.

PAUL: Not really.

LEONARD: We should go up there sometime. We should go up to Whitehorse or somewhere and never come back.

[MINA *enters with sloppy joes, Fritos, and beer.*]

MINA: Soup's on.

LEONARD: Make him stay.

MINA: No, I know that feeling. When it's time to go, it's time to go.

PAUL: It is, thank you.

MINA: On the other hand, I like having you around. [*To* LEONARD] He keeps you out of my hair, at least. [*To* PAUL] Go check on things at the plant, get Ferris from your sister, and bring him back up here next week.

LEONARD: Did you name him after the wheel?

PAUL: Who?

LEONARD: Ferris.

PAUL: No. It was a family name.

LEONARD: My family couldn't afford family names. We just had to settle for whatever our folks could come up with.

MINA: I think this is a good idea. Bring Ferris up here. He can play with Melissa.

[MINA *takes* MELISSA *from* LEONARD.]

Wouldn't that be fun? You could poop on him.

LEONARD: That's all she does.

PAUL: I need to get back in the swing of things!

MINA: This is the swing of things, Paul. I mean, how many people have this kind of freedom; that they can leave their business and visit a little?

LEONARD [*in one flat tone*]: How many people inherit a family business and get everything handed to them on a silver platter just kidding.

PAUL: Very funny.

LEONARD: Really, I love cutting human hair all day, what am I saying, it's my life.

MINA: I mean: this is how friendships die.

LEONARD [*settling back in his seat*]: Exactly.

MINA: We all get so tied down to making a living and keeping things going. Twenty years from now, some little hiccup problem down there at that stupid plant, you won't even remember—but a really good day outside, in the air, with people you love, playing in the snow, coming in, sitting by the fire and talking all night . . . that could be a real day in your life, you know, that you never forget. You wanna miss that?

[*Beat.*]

Stay another week. Just a week; for Winter Carnival. We'll take the snow-mobiles out to Ice Cracking and stay at the cabin. I'll give you lots of chores to do up there. Come on. Not for him. Icky. For me.

PAUL: I don't know . . .

MINA: Come on, I'm supposed to sing next Sunday at Holy Rosary, you could play guitar. It'd be just like back in church camp.

PAUL: Church camp. God. Up in Fertile . . . ?

MINA: Yeah.

[*Beat.*]

PAUL: Do you remember that thing Larry Olsen used to sing . . . ?

[MINA *sings, and* PAUL *haltingly joins in as* LEONARD *watches.*]

PAUL AND MINA [*singing*]: "Be ye kind, one unto another, tender-hearted, forgiving one another, even as God for Christ's sake has forgiven you—doot doo, doodley doo, Ephesians 4:32."

[LEONARD *addresses the audience as* PAUL *and* MINA *freeze.*]

LEONARD: That fucking bitch! Does she honestly think I don't see what's going on here? Or does she not even care? Does she think I'm so stupid I don't notice, or does she think I'm so weak I won't do anything about it? Every night I try to touch her in bed, she says, "Not yet. I'm not ready yet. It's too soon since the baby." I called her fucking doctor, she's ready! She's just not ready to do it with me! And meanwhile she makes special fucking dinners every night for that smiling rich sonofabitch who has the nerve to call himself my friend while he never misses a chance to make me look and feel like a loser. I oughta kill them both with my fucking bare hands.

[*The scene resumes.*]

PAUL: All right. But just for one more week.
MINA [*to* LEONARD]: Happy? Lenny?
LEONARD: Yeah. I'm happy. I'm great.

[LEONARD *takes a big swig of beer.*]

[*To* PAUL] Now you see what I was up against.
MINA: When?
LEONARD [*to* MINA]: When I had you chasing me down all over town back in high school, trying to convince me to marry you—now he can see what I was up against.
MINA: Chasing you down? As I remember it, sir, you asked me to marry you three different times before I finally said yes.
LEONARD: That's not how I remember it.
MINA [*to* PAUL]: He did, he left poems on my desk at the library, he'd spy on me . . .
LEONARD: I never spied on you.
MINA: Yes, he did—
LEONARD: And I never wrote a poem in my life!
MINA [*to* LEONARD]: That's not true, you wrote that poem about the moon landing—
LEONARD: It's not true.

MINA: It was called "One Small Step." [*As if it's precious*] "One Small Step."

LEONARD [*putting a stop to it*]: Anyway, my point was, you're very—persuasive.

MINA: Well, your friend is staying, so whatever I am, you're lucky I'm it.

LEONARD: Yeah. I know. I'm the luckiest man alive.

[LEONARD *rises, pulls out his wallet, pulls out some bills.*]

    Here's your money.

PAUL: Huh?

[LEONARD *hands the money to* PAUL *and gestures at the TV.*]

LEONARD: The game's over.

[*He exits, leaving* PAUL *and* MINA. *A moment passes.*]

PAUL: What the hell just happened?

MINA: I have no idea.

SCENE 3

[LEONARD *and* CARL *are in the barbershop.* LEONARD's *very upset. Note:* CARL *is deaf and communicates primarily with American Sign Language. What matters most is* LEONARD *understands him perfectly and signs back to him along with his own audible speech.*]

LEONARD: Don't lie to me!

CARL: I'm not lying!

LEONARD: I've known you a long time, Carl! I share everything with you every morning I come in here! If I get a pimple on my butt, I tell you!

CARL: That's true.

LEONARD: So don't turn on me now just because it's suddenly cool to talk about me behind my back! What did they say?

CARL: Nothing important!

LEONARD: If they were talking down at Sundberg's Café, I want to know! What'd they say? What?

CARL: Darla Savoy's pregnant again.

LEONARD: Darla Savoy's pregnant, and? What else?

CARL: Angry Dennis painted his tractor blue.

LEONARD [*reading the signs*]: Angry Dennis painted his tractor blue, and no one said a single word about why Paul's suddenly staying an extra week?

CARL: No! Why?

LEONARD: Because he's only staying because he's thinking he's gonna—

[*He makes the sign for sex.*]

—my wife! If he hasn't already!

CARL: That's crazy.

LEONARD: No, it's not crazy; it's perceptive! You know where they are right now?

CARL: No.

LEONARD: At Holy Rosary. He's playing guitar and they're singing, practicing some song they're gonna do in church on Sunday! Singing!

CARL: Singing is not having sex!

LEONARD: It is to women. She's always wished I did something artistic. I know that. She's always thought she was better than me. What a bunch of crap. And Paul's not artistic, anyway! I mean, sure he can play guitar, big deal, that doesn't make you an artist! Any moron with two hands can play guitar!

CARL: Don't be such an asshole!

LEONARD: Don't get outraged at me, Carl, you're probably in on this along with everybody else!

CARL: Stop it! I mean it! Stop! Your wife is the best woman in this whole town—

LEONARD: I know, I know, I'm the luckiest guy in the world—

CARL: You've got a beautiful new daughter—

LEONARD: But is my daughter even mine?

CARL: You need a psychiatrist!

LEONARD: No, I don't need a psychiatrist, I need a gun!

[*Beat.*]

Look, Paul's coming here to meet me. Keep him here for five minutes. You ask him why he's staying and see what he says.

CARL: This is crazy!

LEONARD: Just do it! You're good at reading people. I'll be right back.

CARL: But—

LEONARD: Just do it!!

[LEONARD *pushes past* CARL *and exits.* CARL *turns and addresses the audience, using only ASL.* TIME *appears and translates for the audience.*]

CARL: Shit!

TIME: Expletive deleted.

CARL: I should never have come to work today. He's always been a pain in the butt to work for, but this takes the cake. If I tell Leonard he's right about Paul and Mina—which he's not—who knows what he might do to them? But if I tell Leonard he's wrong, who knows what he'll do to me?

[PAUL *enters.* CARL *senses the motion and sees* PAUL *has come in. Note:* PAUL *signs to* CARL *in ASL and speaks.*]

S—t!

TIME: Expletive deleted.

PAUL: Carl? Do you know what's wrong with Lenny? I just saw him and he walked right by like . . .

[PAUL *removes his hat, scarf, and coat.*]

CARL: It's complicated.

PAUL: He's been begging me to stay, now I'm staying, what's "complicated"?

CARL: Honestly? You should leave town.

PAUL: Leave town? I just said I'd stay. He asked me to stay!

CARL: Just leave town and everything will be OK.

[CARL *puts* PAUL's *coat and scarf back on.*]

PAUL: What the hell are you talking about? What will be OK?

CARL: Give it time.

PAUL: Give what time? What?

[CARL *puts* PAUL's *hat on his head.*]

CARL: Just go. Now. Trust me.

PAUL: But Carl . . .

CARL [*spoken audibly, if possible*]: Trust me!

[*Beat.*]

PAUL: OK.

SCENE 4

[*Music and lights establish a clear, frozen, forbidding winter night. The scene is* LEONARD *and* MINA's *kitchen.* CINDY *is sketching.* MINA *holds the baby and looks out the window.* LINDY *is there, examining a flowerpot with a few green shoots sprouting up. A tense moment passes.*]

CINDY: Do you want me to call down to the Shoreview Pub?

LINDY: No, leave him be.

MINA: Ever since the baby came, it's been like this. I hate it.

LINDY: Well, I'm sure he's feeling the pressure, he's got a family to feed, and Pastor Ed's piece of crap shopping mall downtown isn't making it any easier.

MINA: I know, Lindy, but having a family, having people that love you, isn't that supposed to make things easier? Isn't it?

CINDY: Men don't see it that way, you know that. Honey, sit back down.

[MINA *sits down.* CINDY *sketches* MINA.]

Lindy, I know I said I didn't want any more children, but this little one—

LINDY: Cindy, don't even say it—

CINDY: No, listen, I know we're too old to have one of our own, but—

LINDY: But what?

CINDY: Hold the baby.

LINDY: No.

CINDY: Just hold the baby.

LINDY: No, I'm not gonna hold the baby.

CINDY: Lindy, you hold that baby!

LINDY: Fine, I'll hold the baby.

[LINDY *takes the baby from* MINA.]

MINA: How's my portrait coming?

LINDY: You look like an avocado with hair.

CINDY: Don't listen to him. This is just a study. But when I finally make a real painting of you, it's gonna be my masterpiece.

MINA: *Minnesota Mom*?

LINDY: The *Mama Lisa*.

CINDY: Don't laugh. The Mona Lisa probably was somebody's mom.

LINDY: She didn't look like anybody's mom.

CINDY [*absently, concentrating on drawing*]: Well, I bet she was. When that painting was done, I'm sure some little girl walked up to it at least one time and said, "That's my mom." And then, after a few years went by, I bet someone else looked at it and said, "That's my grandma." "That's my great-grandma." "That's my great-great grandma," and on and on, as if she were suddenly standing right there, alive as you and me. Because art can do that, you know. It can make people last forever. It can bring them back long after time has taken them away. Today, of course, no one remembers the real Mona Lisa, she's just, you know—a masterpiece. But when it all got started, the Mona Lisa was just like Mina. A very pretty lady and somebody's mom.

[LINDY *has wandered over to the flowerpot.*]

LINDY: What are these things?

MINA: Narcissus. I'm forcing them.

CINDY: He's getting bored with his apple trees.

LINDY: I'm not bored. I'm just thinking it might be time to diversify.

MINA: It's really simple to do. You just have to chill them for twelve weeks.

LINDY: And *then* they bloom?

MINA: Yeah. In the basement or somewhere.

LINDY: *After* you chill them?

MINA: Yeah.

LINDY: And what's in there?

MINA: Potting soil, and a little bonemeal.

LINDY: Oh. I don't like that stuff.

MINA: Bonemeal?

LINDY: Yeah. Whose bones, you know what I'm saying? Whose bones?

[*He puts the baby back in* MINA*'s arms.* MINA *goes to the window again to watch for* LEONARD.]

CINDY: So could we maybe adopt one?

LINDY: Yeah, of course, Cindy. Holding the baby for two minutes has completely changed my mind.

CINDY: I'm serious.

LINDY: You've got two grandchildren.

CINDY: I know, but they live so far away.

LINDY: Take a trip, I won't miss you.

CINDY: I wouldn't miss you either.

LINDY: You'd miss me like a fastball down the middle.

CINDY: Honey, why don't you take Lenny to the Fireside Inn next week for your anniversary? Melissa could stay with us. Just send her over with a bottle.

LINDY: Of Scotch.

[*A long pause as* CINDY *and* LINDY *watch* MINA *looking worriedly out the window and then at the baby.*]

CINDY: What are you thinking about? You had a look just then, it was so perfect.

MINA: I was thinking about the minute it happened.

CINDY: When what happened?

MINA: When she was conceived. I know it's probably impossible to know when it happens, but I think I really did. I think I knew when it happened. It was like I was suddenly knit together in a brand new way. Like all my little knots had been undone and then retied in some new pattern by these tiny little hands, all kinda working deep inside me. And radiating out.

CINDY: I remember that feeling.

MINA: We'd been trying for so long, he'd given up, because, you know, that kind of thing drives him crazy. Anything hard, anything boring. But I hadn't given up. I still felt her, you know? I didn't tell him that, but I did, I felt her in the air. I felt her in every room with me, she was my little friend that just hadn't arrived yet. But everywhere was a space she was gonna be. Every little something was a something she was gonna see. Every sunset I looked at, I'd think, "Oh, she would've liked this one. Where is she?"

[*A moment passes.*]

And then one night Lenny came home from work and I'd been reading all day about dreams and I'd fallen asleep in the Warm Room; and I was kinda out of it and the light was strange, like you didn't know if you'd slept all night and just woke up or what time it really was—and, uh, he walked in and came over to me where I was sitting on the daybed and he sat down. So tired. But handsome tired, you know? The good way. And, uh, I could feel the coldness from outside pouring off him and rolling along the edge of the cushion and up under my shirt a little and it felt so good! It felt so fresh, because like I said, I'd been sitting there reading all afternoon, right, and I was so hot because our woodstove is such a creeping disaster, it is, it's the worst thing about this house, but it was one of those moments; one of those moments, you know, when it all becomes finally obvious; when all the details of stupid life fall away for a second and you just know that you're there for each other; that that's why you came. For this rendezvous. And he kissed me. And his face was so cool, and his flannel shirt was so cool, it was like I had snow falling all inside me. I was a snow day.

[*Beat.*]

So still. So quiet. We didn't say a thing. We didn't have to. It was OK. It was that kind of day. And when this special little snowflake landed . . . it was like almost nothing, it was like a dream landing on a dream, landing on a dream . . . but I felt it. I did.

[*A moment passes.*]

And I thought everything was gonna be so nice.

[LEONARD *enters, wearing a heavy coat and gloves.*]

LINDY: Hey, here's the man of the house.
LEONARD: Such as he is, yeah.
CINDY: Hi, Lenny.
LEONARD: Hey, Cindy.
MINA: We held off having dinner as long as we could, where have you been? Did you get stuck in the snow? And you know Paul had to leave, right?
LEONARD: Where's Paul?
MINA: He decided to go home. Something came up.
LEONARD: Is that right? What a shame.

[MINA *offers the baby to* CINDY.]

MINA: Can you take her a second?
CINDY: Sure.

[CINDY *takes the baby.*]

MINA: Yeah, he left a note. I guess he really did need to get back.
LINDY: I hope he's OK on those roads.
LEONARD: Oh, I hope so too. It's dangerous out there.
CINDY: Lindy almost put us in a ditch on the way over, out by Four Corners.
LINDY: I almost put us in a ditch?
CINDY: You were driving.
LINDY: And you were talking.
MINA: So, so where have you been?
LEONARD: None of your fucking business.
CINDY: Lenny . . .
MINA: Have you been at the Shoreview all this time? See, he does, he stinks like the Shoreview, just like I said. Cigarettes and fish.
LINDY: Eau de Shoreview.
MINA: Why don't we get some food in your stomach?

LEONARD: Is it poisoned?

MINA: What?

LEONARD: I said, is it poisoned? Is the food you're gonna give me poisoned?

LINDY: I tasted it all, buddy. You're safe.

LEONARD: I don't feel safe.

MINA: What's that supposed to mean?

LEONARD: Exactly what I said. I don't feel safe in my house.

[*Uncomfortable silence.*]

LINDY: Cindy, should we maybe . . . ?

CINDY: No. Len, I think you oughta do what Mina says, eat something, you'll—

LEONARD: I'm not a little boy.

CINDY: We know you're not, but—

LEONARD: Then stop talking to me, Cindy, like that's what I am when I'm not! You talk to everyone that way, it's so fucking condescending!

LINDY: Take it easy.

[MINA *goes to* CINDY, *who is holding the baby.*]

MINA: Come on, Lenny, please don't make a scene—

LEONARD: Don't tell me what to do!

MINA: If you're gonna start screaming, I'm gonna take the baby away.

LEONARD: Yeah, take the baby away, because I'm such a bad man!

[MINA *takes the baby from* CINDY.]

MINA: Baby, what's the matter?

LEONARD [*to* MINA]: Come here, gimme that thing—

MINA: No, what's the matter with you?

LEONARD: Give it to me, I'll smash her head in!

[LINDY *steps in front of* LEONARD.]

LINDY: All right, let's go outside.

LEONARD: Oh, big man.

LINDY: Come on, we'll get some fresh air.

LEONARD: What a big, tough man.

LINDY: We're just gonna take a little walk.

LEONARD: I don't want to take a little walk!

LINDY: Come on now—

[LINDY *tries to take hold of* LEONARD. *He pulls away and explodes.*]

LEONARD: LEAVE ME ALONE! Everybody leave me alone!

LINDY: What the hell is the matter with you?

LEONARD: She's screwin' around on me! That's what's the matter!

MINA AND CINDY [*not in unison*]: What?

LEONARD: Is that enough? Can I have permission now?

LINDY: Who?

LEONARD: Her! Who do you think?

MINA: Lenny!

LEONARD: Look at her! While I was at that godforsaken barbershop cutting hair every morning, she was—

MINA: What? With who?

LEONARD: Who do you think?

MINA: I don't know what to think!

LEONARD: Paul, you lying bitch, PAUL!

MINA: Lenny, I never—

LEONARD: Don't lie to me!

MINA: I'm not, I don't know how you got this idea—

LEONARD: I got it from—

MINA: Did Paul say something to you? Is this why he left?

LEONARD: You tell me why he left!

MINA: I don't know, did he give you this idea?

LEONARD: No, I got it, I got it from my mind! Because I'm smart and I can see and I can see when things are going on, that's how I got it! By having a brain! Which no one in this town seems to think I have! And maybe I don't have one, considering everyone knew this but me! Carl stood there every day—

[*He scornfully mimes speaking in ASL.*]

—and he knew all the time! Everyone did!

CINDY: Give me the baby and you go get your things.

MINA: No, I'm OK.

CINDY: No, just let him sleep it off—

LEONARD: Like I'm a fever. Like I'm a disease!

LINDY: Lenny, come on, take it easy . . .

LEONARD: I don't have to take standing in my own house being talked about like I'm a disease! I'm the only person who stood up to that sonofabitch!

MINA: Lenny . . .

LEONARD: The only one!

LINDY: Paul?

LEONARD: No, Pastor Ed!

MINA: Lenny—

LEONARD: You know that shopping mall is the biggest mistake this town ever made. You know it wasn't right . . . you knew!

LINDY: I know . . .

LEONARD: But who stood up to him? You? No. Nobody but me. Who made 'em build the whole ugly thing in a circle around my barbershop?

LINDY: You did.

LEONARD: And that spiteful—

MINA: Lenny, please—

LEONARD: Don't interrupt me! That spiteful minister puts a hair salon in the mall right next to me! Don't I have a family? I stick up for what's right and now I don't have a family? I don't have to make a living?

[CINDY *has packed her art supplies in a box and handed them to* LINDY.]

CINDY: Let's go.

MINA: I'm sorry, you guys, just—you're right, go—

CINDY: No, give me the baby and get your things, you're staying with us tonight.

[*A moment while* MINA *decides.*]

MINA: Why are you doing this to us?

LEONARD: Why are YOU doing this to US?

MINA: I'm not doing anything. I haven't done anything for the past six months but stand by you and try to get us all through this.

LEONARD: Through me being a failure.

MINA: No, through, through a really hard time for everybody.

LEONARD: Because of me.

MINA: You know, you love to make this all about you.

LEONARD: Because there's nothing else about me anymore! I'm not making any money! All you care about is the baby!

MINA: That's not true.

LEONARD: Christ, I don't blame you for wanting someone else! Paul's single. He plays guitar! He's got a damn fortune! Go to him!

MINA: I don't want him!

LEONARD: Lie!

MINA: I don't!

LEONARD: Lie!

MINA: I just want us to be happy again! I want us to be a family!

LEONARD: Lie, lie, lie, lie, LIE!

[*A moment passes.*]

MINA: I'm going.

[MINA *goes to exit.* LEONARD *goes after her.*]

LEONARD: Wait a minute, you fucking slut, get back—

[LINDY *stops him.*]

LINDY: Shut the hell up!

LEONARD: I told you: stay out of my way! This is my house!

LINDY: Sit down!

[LEONARD *takes a swing at* LINDY. LINDY *grabs his arm in mid-punch.*]

Lenny, I swear I'll beat the crap outta you if I have to, now leave her alone.
I'll do it. I mean it. I'll do it without a single second thought.

LEONARD: I don't care anyway.

[LEONARD *backs off.*]

CINDY: I'll go help her pack up the baby's things. You keep him out of the way.

[CINDY *exits. A moment passes.*]

LINDY: You know this is all in your head, right? Why are you doing this?

LEONARD: You wouldn't understand.

LINDY: Try me.

LEONARD: No, you wouldn't understand, you're so perfect.

LINDY: I'm not perfect.

LEONARD: Sure you are, you and Cindy are both so perfect with your apple
trees and your art gallery and it's all so nanny-nanny-nanny . . .

LINDY: Hey. She threatens to leave me all the time. We have fights just like
this all the time. Not like this exactly, maybe, but fights. It's a part of life.

LEONARD [*not listening*]: I'll tell you what's part of it, Lindy, part of it is,
there's two kinds of people in this town—

LINDY: That's not true—

LEONARD: Yes, it is, there's north of the tracks and south of the tracks—

LINDY: But you live—

LEONARD: I've never been respected in this town, Lindy, you know that!

LINDY: You're respected! What the hell are you talking about?

LEONARD: Not like you! Not like Cindy! Not like the doctors at the clinic and the lawyers and all those people who belong out to the golf course—

LINDY: So how does this all add up to Paul's sleeping with your wife?

LEONARD: Ask her!

[LEONARD *reaches in his jacket pocket.*]

Don't act like you don't know what I mean, how it all adds up so that when you're laying there on top of your wife, and she's lookin' you in the eye, does she respect you or not, are you a man to her or not, it all adds up, the whole town and everything about life needles down to that one little spot, that one little moment, and you're either . . . a man . . .

[*He pulls a gun from his pocket.*]

LINDY: Lenny . . .

LEONARD: . . . one of the real people . . . or you're not, it's that simple.

[*Without any warning, he puts the gun to the palm of his hand and shoots it. He quickly takes the gun in the other hand and shoots his one good hand right through the palm. He drops the gun to the floor.*]

Ow.

LINDY: Cindy!

CINDY [*offstage*]: What was that sound?

LINDY: Nothing, just, just keep everybody upstairs!

[LEONARD *collapses onto the floor into a seated position.*]

LEONARD: God damn it; that hurts!

LINDY [*preparing to approach*]: Lenny?

LEONARD: WHAT?

[CINDY *enters.*]

CINDY: What is going on down here? Oh, Jesus, Mary, and Joseph.

LINDY: Cindy, when I tell you to keep everybody upstairs, I mean it!

CINDY: Should I call the sheriff?

LINDY: I don't know. Lenny, are you gonna make us have to call the sheriff?

CINDY: I'll call the sheriff.

LINDY: Wouldja just please go upstairs and wait a second? OK?

CINDY: OK.

[*She exits. A moment passes.*]

LINDY: Lenny?
LEONARD: Yeah?
LINDY: I'm gonna come over there and take that gun away, OK?
LEONARD: Yeah.
LINDY: I mean it.
LEONARD: I know.
LINDY: Don't do anything weird.
LEONARD: I won't.

[LINDY *retrieves the gun and steps back.* TIME *is still present, watching.*]

LINDY: I'm gonna send them home in our truck, OK? And then I'm gonna drive you to the hospital. OK? It'll take too long for the ambulance to get out here otherwise. OK?
LEONARD: OK.
LINDY: Cindy! Bring everybody down now! [*To* LEONARD] OK?
LEONARD: OK.

[CINDY *and* MINA *enter, with a suitcase.* MINA *holds the baby.*]

CINDY: Call the sheriff.
LINDY: We're not gonna call the sheriff.
CINDY: He'll find out anyway—
LINDY: Cindy, we're not gonna call the sheriff!
CINDY: Don't talk to me in that tone of voice, mister. You're no better than him when you talk that way.
LINDY: Just take them to our place. I'll take him to the hospital and we'll figure the rest out in the morning. [*To* MINA] Unless *you* want to call the sheriff.
MINA: No.
LINDY [*handing the keys over*]: OK, then. Drive careful. It's slick out there.

[MINA *goes to* LEONARD *and wraps his hands up in towels.*]

MINA: Lenny. Oh, baby. I love you. I don't want anyone but you in my life or touching me ever. You must know that. I have to believe that somewhere in there you still know that. You are everything to me . . . and you have been ever since the day we met. I think you're the most wonderful man in the world and I have always felt so lucky to know you, and the idea that you love me . . . that you love me . . . has always been the most amazing, great surprise of my life.

[*Beat.*]

But I can't let you be a danger to this little girl. I can't do that. I can't. I'm sorry. I can't live this way.

[*She exits past* CINDY. CINDY *seems ready to deliver a speech.*]

LINDY: Don't say anything, please, just get out of here. [*Off her look*] I'm fine!

[CINDY *exits. A moment passes.*]

I've never heard of anybody doing this to themselves before.

[LEONARD *covers his face with his bloody hands and cries.*]

LEONARD: How do you ever be a man? I don't get it, Lindy.

[*He uncovers his bloodstained face, sobbing.*]

How do you ever be a man?

SCENE 5

[*Lights rise on* LEONARD, *asleep in a hospital bed. Both of his hands are thickly bandaged. Seated in a chair by the bed is* MIKE, *a young pastor.* LEONARD *wakes up with a start, as if from a bad dream.*]

LEONARD: Aaggh!
MIKE: It's OK, Mr. Mattson. You're all right.
LEONARD [*shaken*]: Who the hell are you?
MIKE: Mike Goebel.
LEONARD: From First Lutheran . . . ?
MIKE: Yep.
LEONARD: You're the little assistant guy . . . ?
MIKE: Yep.
LEONARD: Where's Pastor Ed? He didn't want to come see me?
MIKE: He didn't think you'd want to see him.
LEONARD: He's right. He's driving me out of business. Since when are ministers supposed to stick their fingers into city planning?
MIKE: I think he thinks it's part of how Christ and culture—
LEONARD: Did he tell you I don't believe in God?

MIKE: He mentioned something about a crisis of faith.

LEONARD: It's not a crisis. Look, Mike. You might as well go. I shot myself. I know what I did. I was upset. It's not a spiritual thing.

[*A moment passes.*]

What? Are you waiting for me to say something else? "I feel so terrible"? "God forgive me for . . . whatever . . . shooting myself"?

MIKE: No. I have some news for you.

LEONARD: Don't tell me, there's another world? Great. Can I have some water?

MIKE: Sure.

[MIKE *holds a glass of water to* LEONARD's *lips. He drinks.*]

LEONARD: Thanks.

[TIME, *who has been standing at a distance, moves closer to* LEONARD.]

So. Give me the news, Mike. Tell me all about the other world.

MIKE: Last night, while your wife and child and Mrs. Linda were driving out to the Lindas', um, after your, um . . .

LEONARD: . . . hand-shooting incident . . .

MIKE: Yep, um . . . it was snowing really hard and they got in an accident at Four Corners, they were hit by a truck coming in from Frazee, your baby's OK, but Mrs. Linda is pretty badly banged up, and your wife is dead.

[*A moment passes.*]

LEONARD: You're kidding.

MIKE: No. I'm sorry, I'm not. In a little bit, they're gonna put you in a wheelchair and take you down to identify her. For legal purposes. But they, they said I should talk to you first.

[*A moment passes.*]

LEONARD: Well, you did it.

MIKE: Do you want me to stay or come with you? Do you want to talk?

LEONARD: No.

MIKE: I'm sure she'd want you to know it's not your fault.

LEONARD: I just said I didn't want to talk, didn't I?

[LEONARD *starts to cry.* MIKE *rises.*]

MIKE: All right. I'll be around the hospital all day, if you need anything. OK.

[MIKE *starts to go.*]

LEONARD: Yeah, wait, I do, hang on. I do need something.
MIKE: What?
LEONARD: Where's Melissa?
MIKE: She's in the nursery, here in the hospital, actually, you want to see her?
LEONARD: No, I don't, listen to me—
MIKE: I'm listening.
LEONARD: Get Carl Kuchenmeister, the deaf fella I work with, and—
MIKE: He's left town, Mister Mattson. [*Off* LEONARD's *look*] I tried to contact him after the accident, while you were still unconscious—
LEONARD: He left town?
MIKE: Yes, sir. He went to Farmington with Mister Anderson; your friend?

[*Beat.*]

LEONARD: OK. All right. I want you to go get that baby—
MIKE: All right—
LEONARD: —and take her to family services or the county or whatever—
MIKE: Mister Mattson, this probably isn't the time to make a decision like—
LEONARD: Is that your job? To tell me when it's time and when it's not?
MIKE: No, but it's my job to, uh, invite you to recognize when—
LEONARD: You don't even know what your job is, do you?
MIKE: I know that it isn't—
LEONARD: Listen, asshole, I'll make it easy for you. If you leave me alone in a house with that baby, I'll kill her. I promise. Because I won't be able to live looking her in the eye after this.
MIKE: That's the way it seems now.

[LEONARD *grabs* MIKE *by the shoulders with his bandaged hands.*]

LEONARD: That's the way it is!

[LEONARD *pulls back.*]

Ow.

[*He holds up his hands; the bandages are newly soaked with blood.*]

There's a word for this, isn't there?
MIKE: I'll go get the doctor—

LEONARD: No, wait! Listen! I'm serious! I want you to go to family services and get me the forms or whatever to give her up, because I can't have her—
MIKE: How about I get the forms and then we talk next week—

[LEONARD *pounds his own face with his bloody bandaged hands.*]

LEONARD: NO NO NO NO NO NO!

[MIKE *grabs* LEONARD's *arms and holds them.*]

MIKE: Mr. Mattson, stop it.
LEONARD: No!

[LEONARD *grabs* MIKE's *face and squeezes his head.*]

You stop it! Get me the forms. Help me figure it out. Or I'll kill her. And then I'll kill myself. I mean it. If anyone brings that little girl in here, I'll break her neck. And what will your precious baby Jesus think of that?

[LEONARD *hits* MIKE *repeatedly.*]

Don't you see I'm trying to do the right thing?
MIKE: Mr. Mattson, let me go!
LEONARD: I'm already dead!
MIKE: In the name of Jesus Christ, I rebuke this spirit of unrest, and I plead—

[LEONARD *locks* MIKE's *head in a headlock and punches him.*]

Help! Somebody help me! Help me!
LEONARD: I'm already dead! I'm already dead!

[LINDY *rushes in and separates them, restrains* LEONARD.]

LINDY: Lenny!
LEONARD [*to* LINDY]: Get him out of here!
MIKE [*to* LINDY]: I'm sorry. This is my first time visiting.
LEONARD: GET OUT!
LINDY: Go on, get out of here. Go get the doctor.

[MIKE *exits.*]

LEONARD: Lindy.
LINDY: What? Come on, settle down, buddy, sit down . . .
LEONARD: Do something with the baby, OK?

LINDY: OK.

LEONARD: No, I mean it. Don't just say OK. Get her away from me. Because I don't know when I'm gonna be ready to . . . I don't know, you know?

LINDY: I'll take care of it. I've got a friend who's got a place in the country—

LEONARD: I don't want to know, OK? I don't. I really don't.

LINDY: OK. I'll take care of it.

LEONARD: I'm not a good father. I know that.

[*Beat.*]

We used to talk, when I'd visit Mina at the library, we used to talk about having kids. Sixteen years old and we'd talk about that stuff. I tied her shoe at Homecoming. In the middle of the dance floor, while everyone else was dancing, I knelt down and tied her shoe. You know? I didn't want her to fall. What's happened to me? I've done everything wrong.

[*Beat.*]

Just . . . make sure that baby's safe and . . . far away from me. OK?

LINDY: OK.

[*Music rises. Lights shift as* LINDY *finds a phone, picks up the earpiece, and dials. In another area, snow begins to fall.*]

Hey, Alec? It's Lindy. Yeah. How's it going down there on the old homestead? We all miss you up here. Yeah. Yeah, it has been a tough winter. A real tough winter. Oh, they're fine. Over a hundred now. Yeah, a hundred apple trees. I know, isn't it? You start out thinking it's gonna be a little project and lo and behold, it turns into something that eats your whole life. Listen. Alec. You like babies, right?

[*Beat.*]

Well, we've got a situation up here.

SCENE 6

[ALEC WILLOUGHBY, *dressed in a heavy coat and hat with earflaps, stands with a baby carriage downstage. He sings to* MELISSA.]

ALEC: YOU, YOU ARE A DREAM JUST WAKING
    YOU ARE A PETAL SHAKING IN THE BREEZE
    YOU, YOU ARE THE FUTURE CALLING

SOFT AS THE SNOW THAT'S FALLING THROUGH THE
    TREES
ALL THINGS SHALL BE NEW
ONCE THEY'RE SEEN BY YOU

YOU'VE COME LIKE A GIFT UNBIDDEN
YOU ARE A SECRET HIDDEN IN A GIRL
HERE, HERE IN MY ARMS SO SILENT
SAFE FROM THIS SAD AND VIOLENT WORLD
YOU WILL TEACH AND LEARN
ALL THINGS TAKE THEIR TURN

BRANCHES BREAK
FLOWERS MAKE
SEEDS AND DIE
BUT SOMETHING DOWN
BENEATH THE GROUND
SEEKS THE SKY

WAIT AND SEE
WAIT AND SEE
THE WORLD TURNS BROWN
BUT STICK AROUND AND IT TURNS GREEN
WAIT AND SEE
WAIT AND SEE
LIFE GETS STRANGE
BUT THINGS CAN CHANGE
WAIT AND SEE

ALEC: Hello Melissa, you little butterfly. My name's Alec. I know this must all seem a little strange to you, but if you end up sticking around for a while, this is not such a bad place to grow up. That over there, see? That's the barn. There are goats in there. And down that way is a lane that goes down to the lake. It's not really much of a lake, but I've got a paddleboat we can take out there in the summer and catch turtles, if you want. And this right here, this field is all white right now because of the snow, but in the springtime, it's like a bomb goes off one day and everything is suddenly blue. Because it's all blue flag iris, as far back as you can see, all the way to the windbreak. Are you OK? You look like you're doing OK. Yeah. Well. This'll be good. We'll have fun.

[*He sings.*]

> YOU HAVE YOUR WHOLE LIFE BEFORE YOU
> DARLING, THIS WORLD WILL FLOOR YOU WITH ITS
>   SIGHTS
> STARS, PLANETS, AND CONSTELLATIONS,
> APPLES AND WHITE CARNATIONS
> AND NORTHERN LIGHTS

[TIME *joins* ALEC *in the song.*]

TIME AND ALEC: ALL WILL BE REVEALED
> IN THIS VERY FIELD

> LOVE WILL BLOOM
> A BRIDE AND GROOM
> WILL MAKE THEIR VOWS

> AND ALL THINGS GRIEVED
> WILL BE RETRIEVED
> I DON'T KNOW HOW
> BUT WAIT AND SEE
> WAIT AND SEE
> THE YEARS WILL FLY
> THE TEARS WILL DRY
> AND THINGS WILL BE AMAZING

> WAIT AND SEE
> WAIT AND SEE
> ALL SHALL BE WELL
> TIME WILL TELL, WAIT AND SEE
ALEC: ALL SHALL BE WELL
> TIME WILL TELL
> WAIT AND SEE.

ACT 2

SCENE 1

[*Lights rise on* TIME. TIME *sings.*]

TIME: WHO AM I
SO SMALL
INVISIBLE AND STRANGE
AND HARDLY HERE AT ALL?

I WANDER
I CREEP
LIKE IVY UP THE WALLS
OF WAKEFULNESS AND SLEEP

UNSEEN BY
LIFE'S EYES
I SNAKE MY SILENT WAY
AND MAKE TRUTH OF ALL THE LIES

LIKE SAND ON A BEACH
SLOWLY FUSING TO GLASS
LIKE A WORD IN A POEM
SEEKING ITS RHYME
I AM TIME
LET ME PASS
LET ME PASS

[*As the song ends, the music turns to pop.* TIME *addresses the audience.*]

TIME: It's eighteen years later. Melissa's all grown up and still living with Alec on the farm. Ferris is grown up, too; he and Melissa are in love, and they don't even know their parents knew each other; hard to believe, but totally true! Carl's working for Paul at the woolen mills in Farmington; Cindy's painting back in Pine City. Leonard's just about to get out of the cuckoo house after eighteen years, and Lindy . . . ?

[LINDY *is chased across the stage by a large* BEAR.]

BEAR: Raaaarrrggghhh!
LINDY: Help! HEEEELLLLPPP!

[LINDY *and the* BEAR *exit.*]

TIME: It's a long story.
MUSICIAN: Five, six, seven, eight!
ALL: EVERYTHING IS COMING UP ROSES AND VIOLETS
EVERYTHING IS COMING UP, IT'S SUDDENLY SPRING
IT'S SUDDENLY SPRING!

EVERYTHING IS SHAKING UP AND BREAKING UP THE
GROUND NOW, EVERYTHING IS WAKING UP,
IT'S SUDDENLY SPRING, IT'S SUDDENLY SPRING!

THE PICTURE-PERFECT SNOW HAS GIVEN WAY TO
GROWING THINGS 'CAUSE THAT'S THE WAY THINGS GO
THEY GROW, THEY GLOW, THEY BLOW AWAY—
THEY LET IT HAPPEN . . .

[PAUL *and* CARL *and* TIME *assemble into a tableau for the next scene as the rest of the cast exits the stage, repeating a vamp.*]

ALL: OOH, AHH, OOH, AHH, SHI-DOOBY
OOH, AHH, OOH, AHH, SHI-DOOBY

SCENE 2

[*Lights immediately shift. Note: in this scene,* CARL *signs to* PAUL, *who understands ASL and is able to sign back, along with talking aloud.*]

PAUL: NO!
CARL: I'll only be gone for a month!
PAUL: I can't spare you for a month! Carl, I can't even spare you for a week!
CARL: Get Ferris to help you out!
PAUL: Ferris? I don't even know where Ferris is half the time anymore, Carl, he's always off somewhere running around with that girl of his. Even if I could get hold of him, he's supposed to be studying for his SATs now, anyway.
CARL: He told me he doesn't want to go to college.
PAUL: Well, he's going to college. He's going to college if I have to take him there and nail him into a chair in the front row of English 101! There are young men all over this country who would give their left nut to go to college. I've got the only one who'd rather—I don't know, what the hell does he say he wants to do now? Grow something?

CARL: Herbs.

PAUL: Herbs. Yeah. Genius. Fresh herbs. There's a million-dollar idea.

CARL: It could be.

PAUL: Planting oregano. He'd rather plant oregano than go to college. Genius! Where does he get these crazy ideas? I thought I raised him right.

CARL: You did!

PAUL: No, I must not have, because it seems like all he wants to do lately is throw everything in my face by doing absolutely nothing with his life!

CARL: Well, you're going to have to figure out how to do without me for a while, because I need to go back to Pine City.

PAUL: Pine City. What do you have to go back there for?

CARL: Leonard's getting out soon—

PAUL: I don't want to talk about Leonard Mattson! He's dead to me. The day we stood there and watched Mina laid in the ground, with him not even there? He belongs in that nuthouse. He should stay there forever.

CARL: I think he's changed.

PAUL: Oh, he's changed? How the hell do you know that?

CARL: Letters. He says he wants to get his life back on track—

PAUL: And what about his daughter, wherever the hell she is? Who's going to get her life back on track? Who knows how screwed up she is, wondering all these years who her real parents are? If she's even alive. Carl, I learned a long time ago when my wife left me and Ferris, romantic love is fine, but being a parent . . . being a parent is the only real relationship there is.

CARL: That's not true.

PAUL: Yes, it is. All the other relationships come out of being a parent. You love your wife because you love your son; you love your husband because you love your daughter; you love what is because you love what might be.

CARL: Not everyone feels that way.

PAUL: Well, it's how I feel. Being a parent, whether it's to a child, or an idea, or anything, being a parent is the only real relationship; you screw that up, you screw up everything. Leonard screwed up everything.

CARL: But if you force your son to go to college when he doesn't want to—

PAUL: Ferris wants to go to college; he just doesn't know it yet! And the day my relationship with MY son becomes your business, I'll let you know!

[PAUL *moves to exit then stops and turns back to* CARL.]

And find that goddamn son of mine! We're gonna settle this matter once and for all.

[PAUL *exits.* CARL *makes a sign to the audience.* TIME *translates.*]

TIME: Expletive deleted.

SCENE 3

[ALEC *is seated, telling a story to* FERRIS, *tying lavender into bundles.* TIME *is present.* MELISSA *is too, but, having heard all this before, is half-listening with her back to the audience, quietly making daisy chains.*]

ALEC: Death. Death. Death. Death. When I was your age, Ferris, that's how I spent my days, that's how I spent my nights. Surrounded by death.

FERRIS: Why?

ALEC: I had to. I was a mortician. It was a family business.

FERRIS: I hate family businesses.

ALEC: They are a little pain-in-the-butt-making, aren't they? See, the problem with family businesses is they tend to be all about the business and not about the family. The family becomes just a, you know, a breeding camp to feed humans into the business, instead of the business being a way to create freedom and opportunity for the family.

FERRIS: It sucks.

ALEC: It does suck. It sucks massively. And it almost sucked me in, too.

FERRIS: What happened?

ALEC: A woman. This woman came to town. She was from Mystic, Connecticut, and she was completely amazing. And she came to Pine City to visit; we met; and she convinced me to get out of the business and do what I wanted.

MELISSA [*filling in* FERRIS, *her back to us*]: Alison.

ALEC: Yeah. Alison Farnham. And so I quit the funeral home, bought this place down here, and Alison and I and this other guy—

FERRIS: Other guy?

ALEC: Yeah, this other guy named Jerry—Alison was pregnant with Jerry's baby, and he was in the Coast Guard, I was in love with her, Jerry was in love with her, and she was in love with both of us. [*Remembering*] One time, the three of us—

MELISSA: Dad!

ALEC: It was kind of a scene.

FERRIS: Sounds like it.

ALEC: Anyway, the plan was we'd all move down here and live together.

FERRIS: Two guys and a girl . . . ?

ALEC: I know! I know. It didn't work out, of course—Jerry . . . died . . .

FERRIS: Oh.

ALEC: Yeah.

FERRIS: But you really would have done it?

ALEC: What? The bunch of us living together?

FERRIS: Yeah.

ALEC: I was willing to try. If Jerry had come back, it probably would have driven him crazy, but . . . we were young, you know? We were kinda loopy.

FERRIS: None of my friends would ever, I mean . . . [*To* MELISSA] I don't think I could share you with anybody.

MELISSA: I wouldn't let you.

[*She kisses him lightly.* TIME *enters operating a puppet butterfly.*]

FERRIS: So then what happened? I mean—

ALEC: Well, after a few years, Alison moved to San Francisco, because she'd always wanted to do that. So that left me here, all alone, and I thought everything had gone kinda wrong. Which is what you think when you're young. That things can go wrong. But sometimes things going wrong is just life getting ready to blow your mind, you know? Because then, one snowy night, I'm all alone; and this baby basically showed up at my door.

[TIME *and the butterfly flutter over near* ALEC.]

She was from way up north. And a little bit out of her natural range. Just like this little lady.

[*He holds out his hand, but the butterfly lands on* ALEC's *hat.*]

Melissa Arctic.

[*A moment passes, and the butterfly takes off.*]

And my life has been like a fairy tale ever since. Just think about it, Ferris. I started out as a mortician, and now I get to be around all this life. I get to know her and you and . . . everybody. What a . . . chance, you know? What a chance it is to be in the world.

[*Beat.*]

FERRIS [*getting an idea*]: Mister Willoughby?

ALEC: Yup . . . ?

FERRIS: Do you think I should go to college like my dad wants?

ALEC: Ferris, my boy. You know what the secret to life is?

FERRIS: What?

ALEC: No one can tell anyone anything.

[ALEC *prepares to exit.*]

So, are you two planning on doing anything useful for me today, or are you just gonna sit out here and play or whatever it is you two do?

FERRIS: We'll bring all that lavender up to the barn.

MELISSA: In a little bit.

FERRIS: In a little bit.

ALEC: Great. You coming with us to the farmers' market this weekend? It's the county fair. There'll be rides and stuff. And a dance.

FERRIS: If she wants me to.

[*Beat.*]

MELISSA: Sure.

FERRIS: Then I'll come.

ALEC: You be good to my little girl, OK?

FERRIS: I will, sir.

[ALEC *starts to exit.*]

ALEC: Have either of you guys seen the cat?

FERRIS AND MELISSA [*not in unison*]: No.

ALEC: That little guy wanders off so much, I swear, I'm gonna change his name to Ulysses. Ulysses Kitty.

[ALEC *heads away, whistling.*]

Here, kitty, kitty . . .

[*A moment passes.* MELISSA *turns to face* FERRIS.]

FERRIS: Your dad's cool.

MELISSA: He's fine. He's a little out of it.

[*She takes a pamphlet and a watch from her pocket.*]

FERRIS: What's that?

MELISSA: I want to do something.

FERRIS: What?

MELISSA: Sit up. Across from me. Here.

FERRIS: What are we doing?

MELISSA: You'll see.

FERRIS: What's the watch for?

MELISSA: I was looking around in the attic for a dress to wear to the dance this weekend, and I found an old chest, it must have been Alison's. It had all kinds of books and stuff in it. And it had this little pamphlet . . .

FERRIS: About what?

MELISSA: How to hypnotize people.

FERRIS: I can't be hypnotized.

MELISSA: You wanna bet?

FERRIS: Why would you want to hypnotize me, anyway? I'll do whatever you want.

MELISSA: Just let me try and hypnotize you. OK?

FERRIS: OK. But it's not gonna work.

MELISSA: We'll see about that.

[*Music begins—a dreamy pentatonic lullaby.*]

Are you in a comfortable position?

FERRIS: Yeah.

MELISSA: And are you willing? Because it says you have to be willing.

FERRIS: I'm willing.

MELISSA: You have to be really willing.

FERRIS: I'm willing now! I'm really willing!

[*Beat.*]

I'm willing.

MELISSA: OK.

[*The musical arrangement clarifies as* MELISSA *begins swinging the watch back and forth in front of* FERRIS*'s eyes.* MELISSA *sings.*]

YOU'RE GETTING SLEEPY.
YOU'RE FEELING VERY TIRED,
STARTING TO UNWIND AND FIND A KIND OF
DEEP PEACEFULNESS.
Now repeat after me . . .

MELISSA AND FERRIS: YOU'RE [I'M] GETTING SLEEPY.
YOU'RE [I'M] FEELING VERY TIRED,
STARTING TO UNWIND AND FIND A KIND OF
DEEP PEACEFULNESS.

[*Then the music falls to low accompaniment.* FERRIS*'s eyes are closed.*]

MELISSA: Ferris?

[*Beat.*]

Can you hear me?

FERRIS [*trance-like*]: Yes.

MELISSA: Are you hypnotized?

FERRIS: I think so.

MELISSA: Lift up your right hand.

[*He does so.*]

OK, put it down now.

[*He does so.*]

OK. Now . . . I'm going to tell you something now, and I want you to do exactly what I say, OK? Say, "I'll do exactly what you say."

FERRIS: I'll do exactly what you say.

MELISSA: OK. When you wake up from this trance, you will leave this farm and never come back here again. Because you have a good future ahead of you. You should go to college out East like your father wants. You should get out of Minnesota and do something with your life. Do you understand?

FERRIS: Yes.

MELISSA: And I'm going to stay here, because this is where I like to be. I can't leave these fields and flowers for more than a day without feeling all cold and dead inside. I wish it was different, but it isn't. You have to go.

FERRIS: I have to go.

MELISSA: And I have to stay.

FERRIS: You have to stay.

MELISSA: Now, when you wake up, you'll think of me as a good friend . . .

FERRIS: . . . you're a good friend . . .

MELISSA: . . . and you'll tell me that you've decided to go to college out East and that you promise to write. But then you won't ever write, OK?

FERRIS: I won't ever write.

MELISSA: Because that would be too hard for me, OK?

FERRIS: I won't ever write.

MELISSA: Promise.

FERRIS: I promise I won't ever write.

MELISSA: OK.

[*She looks at him awhile. Then she gathers up her resolve.*]

Now, I'm going to dehypnotize you, and when you wake up, you won't remember a thing. OK?
FERRIS: OK.

[*Music rises. She sings.*]

MELISSA: YOU'RE SLOWLY WAKING.
YOU'RE RISING THROUGH A MIST,
HIGH ABOVE THE MAZE OF LAZY DAYS AND
DEEP PEACEFULNESS.
Now, repeat after me.

[*As* MELISSA *sings the preceding verse,* FERRIS *sings back the subsequent verse.* TIME *takes the watch from her and swings it between the two lovers.*]

MELISSA: YOU'RE SLOWLY WAKING. YOU'RE RISING THROUGH A MIST, HIGH ABOVE THE MAZE OF LAZY DAYS AND DEEP PEACEFULNESS

FERRIS: YOU'RE GETTING SLEEPY YOU'RE FEELING VERY TIRED STARTING TO UNWIND AND FIND A KIND OF DEEP PEACEFULNESS

[MELISSA *closes her eyes and falls into a trance.*]

FERRIS: Melissa?

[*Beat.*]

Can you hear me?
MELISSA: Yes.
FERRIS: Are you hypnotized?
MELISSA: I think so.
FERRIS: Touch your nose.

[*She does so.*]

Good. Put your hand down now.

[*She does so.*]

Now listen. I don't want to go to college. I don't want to go into business, I want to spend the rest of my life with you, right here. I want to kiss you and hold you and marry you and rush to the hospital and hold your hand while you have babies and I want to give you everything you want and take long walks and get old and be your best friend forever. OK?

MELISSA: OK.

FERRIS: So when you wake up from this trance, I want you to forget all about trying to hypnotize me, and when I take a ring out of my shirt pocket and ask you to marry me, I want you to say yes and then that will be the end of it. Do you understand?

MELISSA: Yes.

FERRIS: Do you really understand?

MELISSA: Yes. I really understand.

FERRIS: Because I don't want to live on earth without you.

[*He looks at her awhile.*]

OK, I'm going to dehypnotize you now, and when you wake up, you won't remember any of this happened.

[*Music rises.*]

YOU'RE SLOWLY WAKING.
YOU'RE RISING THROUGH A MIST,
HIGH ABOVE THE MAZE OF LAZY DAYS AND
DEEP PEACEFULNESS.

[*The music ends.* TIME *takes the watch, pockets it, and steps back into the flowers. A long moment passes.*]

MELISSA: It's a nice day, isn't it . . . ?

FERRIS: Sure is.

MELISSA [*unsure*]: So . . . we should take the lavender . . . bring it up to the . . . ?

FERRIS: Yeah, but wait a second. I want to give you something.

[*He starts to reach into his shirt pocket. She stops him and grabs him by the shoulders, looking him right in the eye.*]

MELISSA [*responding to his about-to-be-uttered proposal*]: YES!

[*A moment of recognition. They kiss.*]

SCENE 4

[*After a brief tableau, the farmers' market springs to life.* ALEC, FERRIS, *and* MELISSA *are all at a flower and herb stand.*]

ALEC: Do you guys want some coffee? Mini-doughnuts? Pork chop on a stick?

FERRIS: I'll get you some coffee, Mr. Willoughby.

ALEC: OK. Here, take a little money.

FERRIS: No, that's all right. I'll get it. But thank you.

[FERRIS *exits.* PAUL *and* CARL *enter.* PAUL'*s fuming.*]

PAUL: Look at this. A farmers' market . . . ? What the hell is he thinking?

CARL: Go easy on him.

PAUL: Yeah, I'll go easy on him all the way to the woodshed!

[PAUL *and* CARL *arrive at the flower stand.*]

   Mr. Willoughby?

ALEC: Yes, sir.

PAUL: I'm Paul Anderson. Ferris Anderson's father.

ALEC: Oh, wow! Pleased to meet you. You've got a fine young man for a son.

PAUL: I think so, too, did he—

ALEC: He's always such a big help out at our place. I don't remember being that responsible when I was a kid, unless somebody made me.

PAUL: Exactly. Did he happen to—

ALEC: Who's your friend?

PAUL [*having been gazing at* MELISSA]: Oh, this is Carl Kuchenmeister. He runs the woolen mill with me. I'm basically a figurehead.

ALEC: Kuchenmeister. What a fun name. Pleased to meet you.

[ALEC *and* CARL *shake hands.*]

PAUL: He's deaf.

ALEC: Oh! Wow! [*To* CARL, *loudly, as they shake hands*] That must be interesting!

CARL: No more interesting than your life.

ALEC [*to* PAUL]: What did he just say?

PAUL: He says it's no more interesting than your life.

CARL: Maybe less, because I sit at a desk all day inside a factory while you get to run around outside with all these flowers.

PAUL: Ferris didn't—

ALEC [*to* PAUL]: I'm sorry, Paul, what is that he is saying, that's so fascinating what he's doing there with his—you know, with his hands—

PAUL [*impatient*]: Mr. Willoughby! Did Ferris come with you this morning?

ALEC: As a matter of fact, he did.

PAUL: So where the hell is he?

ALEC: Uhh, he went to get me some coffee. Is something wrong?

PAUL: Well, actually, yes—

ALEC: I mean, I hope I didn't do anything wrong, he said he had permission—

PAUL: But he *would* say that, wouldn't he?

[FERRIS *and* MELISSA *enter with a pork chop on a stick.*]

FERRIS: I got you a pork chop on a stick, Mr.—Dad!

PAUL: What are you doing here?

FERRIS: What are *you* doing here?

PAUL: You don't know? You're honestly willing to pretend you don't know?

FERRIS: I—I'm not sure what you mean—

PAUL: Where are you supposed to be this morning?

FERRIS: Supposed to be? Where's anybody supposed to be?

ALEC: [*sotto voce*]: Right on.

PAUL [*to* ALEC]: Shut up! [*To* FERRIS] Don't treat me like I'm an idiot! You're supposed to be at St. Olaf in ten minutes to take your SATs and you know it!

FERRIS: I forgot!

PAUL: You did not forget!

FERRIS: Yes, I did!

PAUL: Don't lie! You disobeyed me! Don't you understand, you have to take that test if you want to get into college ... ?

FERRIS: Yeah, but I don't want to take it! I don't even want to go to college!

PAUL: You want to do this? You want to sell flowers?

FERRIS: Herbs, Dad! Herbs!

PAUL: Herbs, whatever!

FERRIS: No, Dad, not "whatever"! These are flowers and these are herbs!

PAUL: Either way, you want to live like this?

ALEC: It's not so bad.

PAUL: I'm sure it isn't, for you, Mr. Whatever-Your-Name-Is, that's wonderful, but I was hoping my son could have a little bit more—

FERRIS: What, Dad? Money? Self-righteousness?

PAUL: Don't talk to me in that tone of voice, young man.

FERRIS: I'll talk to you however I want!

[PAUL *slaps* FERRIS *hard.* EVERYONE'S *shocked.*]

ALEC [*sotto voce*]: He hits the kid ...

PAUL [*to* ALEC]: I told you, shut the hell up! This is none of your business! [*To* FERRIS] I have tried my best to raise you and give you everything you need—

FERRIS: —and make me just like you so I could run your stupid company!

PAUL: Don't finish my sentences! I've tried to give you all the advantages and choices that I didn't have because I DIDN'T want you to have to run that godforsaken mill just because the family said so! I want you to be free!

FERRIS: And I am! I am free!

PAUL: You are!

FERRIS: I am!

PAUL: Yeah, as of right now, you're totally free! When you get back to the house tonight, you'll find all your things packed up, I want you out of my house.

FERRIS: OK.

PAUL: Don't say OK! Don't say anything! [*To* CARL] I'm through with him!

CARL [*signing, to* PAUL]: You need to calm down.

PAUL [*to* CARL]: Shut up, Carl! [*To* FERRIS] And where do you think you're going to get money for your stupid herb farm? [*Gesturing to* ALEC] This dope? This hayseed?

MELISSA: You know, you're really being kind of a—

ALEC [*to* MELISSA]: Whoa whoa whoa ...

PAUL: Where do you think you'll get anything after you've treated me like this? Come on, Carl, let's go.

[CARL *doesn't move.* PAUL *almost exits then turns.*]

[*To* ALEC *and* MELISSA] I'm sorry if I've said anything—disrespectful. If I did, it was inadvertent. I'm sure you're very nice people and there's nothing technically wrong with—growing things. [*To* CARL] Are you coming?

CARL [*signing to* PAUL]: In a minute.

[PAUL *goes to* FERRIS.]

PAUL: From the minute you were born, your mother didn't know what the hell to do with you. I used to think she was crazy. Now I'm not so sure.

[PAUL *storms out.* CARL *and* FERRIS *speak and sign.*]

FERRIS: Why is he like that? Why?

CARL: He loves you very much. He just doesn't know how to show it.

FERRIS: He doesn't love me.

CARL: Yes, he does.

FERRIS: Well, so what, it doesn't matter. I hate him.

CARL: You're a lot like him. Be careful who you hate.

FERRIS: Can I stay with you for a few days? Until—

MELISSA: You can stay with us. Right, Dad?

ALEC: Fine with me.

MELISSA [*trying to sign*]: He can stay with us.

CARL: Wait! Wait a second!

FERRIS: What?

CARL: What's her name?

FERRIS [*gesturing to* MELISSA]: Who? Her?

CARL: Yes.

FERRIS [*spoken and finger-spelled*]: Melissa.

MELISSA: Hi.

[CARL *takes a beat and realizes who* MELISSA *is.*]

CARL [*to* FERRIS]: Do me a favor. Ask him if he knew someone, once upon a time, named Lindy.

FERRIS [*to* ALEC]: He wants to know if you knew someone, "once upon a time," named Lindy?

ALEC: Yeah. "Once upon a time."

[CARL *looks at* MELISSA *for a moment and then turns to* FERRIS.]

CARL: Here's what I think you should do. Take my car and go to Pine City.

FERRIS: Pine City? Up north?

CARL: Yes. Both of you.

FERRIS: My dad just threw me out of the house, and we're supposed to go to Pine City?

MELISSA: We don't know anybody in Pine City!

ALEC: Yes, you do. Trust me.

MELISSA [*to* CARL]: OK.

[CARL *drops the car keys into* MELISSA'*s hand.*]

SCENE 5

[CINDY, LEONARD, *and* TIME *are in* CINDY's *art gallery.*]

CINDY: Do you think that painting's not in the right place?

LEONARD: No, it looks pretty where it is. It could look good there, too, though.

CINDY: No. I'm saving that wall for something special.

LEONARD [*after a look*]: It's good where it is.

CINDY [*after a look*]: I can wait to decide, I guess. The opening's not till tomorrow night.

[*Beat.*]

That one just doesn't feel at home yet.

[LEONARD *wanders over to another painting.*]

LEONARD: Is that the Pavilion?

CINDY: Yep.

LEONARD: God. We had some fun times there, didn't we?

CINDY: We sure did. Homecoming. Prom. Summer Carnival.

LEONARD: And there's Sundberg's Café. [*With melancholy import*] The Shoreview.

CINDY [*trying to make it better, pointing to different paintings*]: Yeah, the Shoreview; the Sandwich Hut; Lindy; the whole town's in here.

LEONARD: Except for Mina.

[*Brief pause.*]

CINDY: Lenny, at some point you have to let her go.

LEONARD: I can't.

CINDY: You have to.

LEONARD: I don't want to.

CINDY: I think what you don't want to let go of is hating yourself.

LEONARD: Maybe hating myself is the only way I have left to love her.

CINDY: Maybe hating yourself is the only way you can *keep* from loving her as much as you know you want to.

LEONARD: She's gone.

CINDY: That doesn't matter. Love doesn't know she's gone. Love just loves. And it wants to keep loving.

LEONARD: When did you get so smart?

CINDY: I'm not smart. You know what I do every night before I go to bed? I lock up the house and turn off all the lights. But I leave the light on over the stove because . . . you know why? It's the dumbest thing. Lindy used to wake up every night around three in the morning, he couldn't sleep through the night, he never could. And he used to go downstairs and make himself a cup of tea and he and Sanka—you remember that dog?

LEONARD: No.

CINDY: He and Sanka would sit there on the kitchen floor and he'd do yesterday's crossword, waiting for the morning paper to be delivered. And so I'd always leave the light on for him down there. Almost twenty years he's gone, and I'm still leaving a light on for him . . . ? Does that sound like someone who's smart to you? Someone who doesn't even know the difference between dead and alive?

LEONARD: I still dream about Mina.

CINDY: Oh, dreams, don't even get me started. You don't know. Lindy and I still have arguments walking out under the apple trees in the sunshine. Big arguments.

LEONARD: I always see her just before she walked out the door. Like a picture in my head.

[CINDY *and* LEONARD *are lost in their own private reveries. He sings.*]

HOW DO YOU START?
HOW DO YOU STEP
INTO THE DARK
WHERE YOU'VE NEVER BEEN?

HOW DO YOU GROW?
HOW DO YOU CHANGE?
HOW DO YOU KNOW
WHICH DIRECTION TO GO?

IT'S SO STRANGE TO LIVE MORE
THAN A LITTLE WHILE
CINDY: HOW DO YOU LOVE
ALL THAT YOU'VE BEEN
AND THEN LET IT GO
SO LIFE CAN BEGIN?

HOW DO YOU GIVE
INTO THE TRUE

THAT WANTS TO BECOME
THE NEW PART OF YOU?

IT'S SO HARD TO LIVE MORE
THAN A LITTLE WHILE
TIME [*chiming in, to make a trio*]: THIS MUST BE
THIS MUST BE WHY PEOPLE PRAY
THIS MUST BE
THIS MUST BE WHY PEOPLE SAY
TO THE SKY AND THE STARS
CINDY AND LEONARD: HOW DO I START?
HOW DO I STEP
INTO THE DARK
WHERE I'VE NEVER BEEN?

HOW DO I GROW?
HOW DO I CHANGE?
HOW DO I KNOW
WHICH DIRECTION TO GO?

IT'S SO STRANGE TO LIVE MORE
THAN A LITTLE WHILE
WHEN YOU WANT TO LIVE MORE
THAN A LITTLE WHILE

[FERRIS *and* MELISSA *enter.*]

FERRIS: Mrs. . . . Linda?
CINDY: That's me. We're kinda closed now—there's an opening tomorrow if
    you want, though, with lemonade and everything, it should be kinda fun—
FERRIS: No, I came—
CINDY: There's some postcards by the door—
FERRIS: No, Mr. Kuchenmeister told me to come.
LEONARD: Carl Kuchenmeister? The . . . deaf fella?
FERRIS: Yeah.
LEONARD: And who are you?
FERRIS: I'm Ferris Anderson.
LEONARD: Paul Anderson's boy . . . ?
FERRIS: Yeah.

[LEONARD *just stands there, unable to go on.* CINDY *takes over.*]

CINDY: And who's this?

[FERRIS *fumbles for what to say.*]

FERRIS: This is my Queen of Everything That's Beautiful and Good.
CINDY: Oh! Nice to meet you.

[CINDY *and* MELISSA *shake hands.*]

MELISSA: You can call me Melissa.
CINDY: Melissa . . . ?

[MELISSA *notices* LEONARD *looking at her.*]

MELISSA: What? Everybody's looking at me funny lately. [*To* LEONARD]
    What are you looking at? [*To* CINDY] What's he looking at?
CINDY: Art.

[*Music rises, lights shift.*]

SCENE 6

[THREE FISHERMEN (*played by the actors playing* MIKE, LINDY, *and* TIME,
in that order) *appear, fishing.*]

1: Did you hear what happened down at Sundberg's Café last night?
2: Angry Dennis came in with a gun and got himself arrested, I know.
1: You're kidding me.
2: No. He's still upset Katie Hoekstra won't marry him.
1: She's fifteen years old!
2: Tell him. He's painted her name all over the side of his house with that crazy
    blue paint he likes so much. He puts that stuff all over everything.
3: What'd he have?
2: To eat?
3: Yeah.
1: What does it matter what he had? He had a gun! That's what he had!
3: I got a theory.
2: You got a theory? About what?
3: I'm not gonna tell you, because I don't like your tone.
1 [*to* 2]: Anyhow, that's not what I was gonna tell you. You remember Paul
    Anderson?
2: Which one? The Wiggler?

1: No, the other one. Owns the woolen mills down in Farmington.

2: Oh yeah.

1: *His* grown boy and his boy's little girlfriend from Farmington come into the café with Leonard Mattson . . .

2: Holy crap.

1: I know.

3: What'd they have?

2: *To eat?*

3: Yeah. [*To* 1] Were you there?

1: What the hell difference can it possibly make what they ate?

3 [*to* 1]: Were you there?

1: I'm not even gonna answer that question, it's too oblique! [*To* 2] So they come in with Leonard, who's just out of the chicken coop after seventeen-some years because of that whole business with Paul and his wife, right? With that jealousy situation? And they sit down and start eating . . .

[*A moment passes as* 1 *and* 2 *wait for* 3 *to interrupt.*]

Until in walks Paul Anderson, and who's *he* got with him but Carl Kuchenmeister—

2: That deaf fella that used to cut hair with Leonard?

1: Yeah, until he took off because of the thing, there was some business about a gun or something . . .

2: Yeah, that was when Lindy died.

1: He didn't get shot by Leonard.

2: No, but after Mina died, he took that little baby off somewhere, remember? And on the way back up, he got killed by that bear.

1: That's, that's a bunch of crap.

2: No! He got out to pee near New Munich and got attacked by a bear that was eating a deer in a ditch. I heard it from a friend of mine in the Highway Patrol.

1: You're kidding me.

2: No, it's like there've been seven bear-related deaths in Minnesota in the past hundred years and that was one. But what, still, nobody knows is, whatever happened to that baby.

1: That's what I'm trying to tell you!

3: The bear was eating a deer . . .

2: You know, you gotta stop.

1: Anyway, so, Leonard and these two kids are sitting down to dinner and I guess Carl was the one who sent 'em up this way because of some trouble with the dad, and it turns out *she's* the baby, *she's* Leonard's little girl.

2: Holy crap.

1: I know. Sitting right there at Sundberg's.

3: What'd they have?

1 AND 2: It doesn't matter what they had!

3: And what if it did? Would you know? Would you be aware? Would you be even willing to see there's something going on in this world you don't know about? Something invisible and constructive and real?

2: You're a moron.

3: Maybe I am. And maybe I'm not.

2: So she's the baby.

1: Yes. *And* she's the sweetheart of Paul's boy to the point where they're all set to get hitched, and the whole bunch of 'em were never aware, and so Paul comes in off the road from following him up here, all full of piss and vinegar and ready to kick the boy's butt, and who does he see but Leonard Mattson sitting there and all hell breaks loose!

2: What do you mean?

1: Everyone starts . . . crying!

2: Holy crap.

1: I know! They start crying and hugging and pretty soon everybody in the whole place was crying, it was nuts!

2: The whole place!

1: I know! Customers, waitresses . . . the town's never seen anything like it. A whole restaurant full of people, weeping.

2: So what happened?

1: What do you think? They all sat down and had dinner together.

3: What'd they have?

1: Leonard had meat loaf, Paul had the half chicken, Carl had vegetable beef soup and a salad, no dressing, the girl had walleye, the boy had the pot pie special and a hamburger, they all shared two large orders of fries, and a whole apple pie for dessert with coffee for everybody. OK?

3: I see things you dopeheads don't see.

1: Uh-huh.

3: There are forces at work.

2: So what's gonna happen?

1: I don't know, I guess they're all staying out to Leonard's and getting ready for tonight.
2: What's going on tonight?
1: Cindy Linda's got an opening at that art center of hers, says she's gonna unveil her masterpiece, a painting of Mina Mattson. No one's ever seen it.
2: Holy crap.
1: I know.

[*A moment passes.*]

2: Life'll really come and get you if you don't be careful, won't it?
1: It sure as hell will.

[*A moment passes.*]

3: It's too bad about Lindy, though.
1: Yeah it is.
3: I wouldn't want to be eaten by a bear.
2: Me neither.
3: To look into that bear's eyes while he's chomping away on your guts . . . ?
2: You'd hopefully go into shock or something.
3: And then all the waiting.

[*Brief pause.*]

1: I for one don't think he really got eaten by a bear.
2 AND 3: So where is he?

[*Brief pause.*]

1: Good point.

[*Music rises as scene shifts.*]

SCENE 7

[*As with all the scenes, lights rise as though upon a painting. Present are* CINDY, LEONARD, FERRIS, PAUL, ALEC, CARL, MELISSA, *and* TIME. ALL *are milling about, looking at various paintings, chatting. They're all frozen. Suddenly,* FERRIS, LEONARD, *and* MELISSA *spring to life.*]

FERRIS: So what's it like in a mental hospital.
MELISSA [*shocked, disapproving*]: Ferris!

LEONARD: It's all right.

FERRIS: Is it really bizarre?

LEONARD: No. It's really boring.

FERRIS: Boring?

LEONARD: Yeah, it's unbelievably boring.

FERRIS: Why?

LEONARD: Because everybody's crazy! They're not in the world, they're not in ... reality.

[*Beat.*]

Reality's bizarre. Being crazy is just ... boring.

FERRIS: By comparison.

LEONARD: Yeah. That's just my opinion, though. And I'm crazy.

[*Focus shifts to* CINDY *and* CARL. CINDY *is wearing a pretty dress.*]

CINDY [*referring to the dress*]: You really think it looks OK?

CARL: Yes. It looks beautiful.

CINDY: I haven't pulled this thing out in years, but I felt like tonight might be special. I don't know.

CARL: You look like an angel.

CINDY: Like what?

[CARL *shows her the sign as he speaks.*]

CARL: Like an *angel.*

CINDY: Oh. Thank you.

[*Focus shifts to* ALEC *and* PAUL.]

PAUL [*does school cheer*]: "Pine City Panthers on the prowl. Gonna getya. Gonna getya. Hear us growl!"

ALEC: Grrr.

PAUL: Alec, we went to school together, how could we not know each other?

ALEC: Nobody knew me. And I didn't know anybody. I was a mortician. I came and went. I didn't go to dances. I didn't talk to anybody.

PAUL [*piecing together the concept*]: So you ... you're in my senior yearbook?

ALEC: No. No. I missed picture day that year. A guy fell into a cheese vat in Vergas and got all sliced up. I had to skip out after English and deal with it.

[*Beat.*]

[*As though it's obvious*] You know, that blade, it just goes around and around.

[*Beat.*]

That's what got me off cheese.

PAUL: It would, wouldn't it.

ALEC: Oh yeah.

[*The* MUSICIAN *plays one last annunciatory flourish.*]

CINDY: Everybody! Everybody gather round, please.

[ALL *gather near the "painting." The rest is restructured or new.*]

CINDY: Thank you for coming. Tonight is a very special night, because by the grace of whatever it is that moves the sun and the stars around, a lot of very good old friends are back together again after way too long. And if all my paintings ever turn out to be good for is this, you know, bringing people together, being a reason for all of us—painted and unpainted—to see each other after all these years . . . well then, every minute I spent dragging a brush across a canvas was worth it.

ALEC: Right on.

[*Everyone claps.*]

LEONARD [*with trepidation*]: So, Cindy, can we see this, uh, this masterpiece of yours?

CINDY [*with equal trepidation*]: OK. Yeah. Sure.

[CINDY *mimes unveiling the painting, which hangs on the invisible fourth wall.*]

There she is. [*To* LEONARD] What do you think?

MELISSA [*quietly, to herself*]: Oh my God.

[FERRIS *puts an arm around* MELISSA. LEONARD *approaches the painting. Beat.*]

FERRIS: Does it look like her?

LEONARD: Yeah. It looks like her.

[MELISSA *moves to* LEONARD *but focuses on the painting.*]

MELISSA: She was so pretty.

LEONARD: Yeah. She was beautiful.

[LEONARD, *very moved by seeing the painting, addresses the group.*]

You know, there were so many times, you guys, sitting up in that place, when I thought I'd never see any of you again.

CINDY [*referring to his emotion*]: It's OK, Lenny . . .

LEONARD: Cindy visited me a lot, but you, Paul . . . Carl . . . Alec, I don't really know you but, hey—

ALEC: Hey—

LEONARD: Thank you so much for—for everything.

ALEC: Leonard, believe me—[*referring to* MELISSA]—it was my pleasure.

LEONARD: Ferris . . . Melissa. I can't . . . I just can't tell you how lucky I feel to have you all back in my life, even just a little, even if it's just for tonight. After all the stupid things I've done, being in your company tonight is a blessing I don't deserve.

PAUL: That's why they call them "blessings," Lenny. No one "deserves" them. They just happen. [*After a look to* FERRIS, *moved*] Like this son of mine . . . right?

LEONARD: Right.

PAUL: I mean, who deserves a son this good? Me? No. It just happened.

[FERRIS *moves closer to* PAUL. LEONARD *looks back at the "painting."*]

LEONARD [*to* MELISSA]: I used to go to the library, where she worked during high school, and I'd spy on her. From between the stacks. Remember that, Paul?

PAUL: Yeah.

[*Beat.*]

LEONARD: I did chase her down, you know? I did. And I always used to joke about it—you remember, Paul?—I'd always pretend I didn't. But I did. She was life to me, pure and simple, and I just had to be near her.

[*Beat.*]

[*Moved*] Why did I make a joke about it? Why did I pretend it wasn't true when it was the only good thing I ever did?

CINDY: Lenny, it wasn't the only good thing you ever did.

[MELISSA *steps closer to the "painting."*]

MELISSA: I wish I could have known her.

LEONARD: I wish you could have, too.

MELISSA: It would be so much fun to sit down with her and tell her all the stuff I've seen. I always wanted to do that. I've always wanted to tell her about the people I know, and what I'm doing. I don't know why that would matter, but it does. I guess I want her to see me. [*To* CINDY] Is it too strange if I ...?

CINDY: What?

MELISSA: Can I say something to her?

CINDY: Go ahead.

[*A moment passes.*]

MELISSA: Mom?

[*Music for "Everything Be Still" starts.*]

It's been ... it's been really great being alive. I read a lot of books and I spend a lot of time outside. Because I like the sun. And I like music, it's really fun to sing songs, and I play piano. I'm not great, but I'm OK. And I'm in love! And I just wish we could have been friends; instead of the way it was.

TIME: EVERYTHING BE STILL ...

[*Everyone moves closer to* MELISSA *and the "painting," finding positions close to the people they need the most right this moment.*]

MELISSA [*to* CINDY, *amazed, referring to the painting*]: That's my mom.

CINDY [*aware of the echo*]: That's your mom.

TIME: EVERYTHING BE STILL ...

MELISSA [*to* LEONARD]: I feel like she sees me.

[*Beat.*]

I feel seen.

LEONARD: You are.

[*He puts an arm gently, humbly, around her.*]

You are.

[*Everyone moves closer, gathering in a semicircular cloud around* MELISSA, *facing* TIME, *who's been standing with its back to us throughout.*]

TIME [*singing*]: CAN EVERYTHING BE PERFECTLY STILL?

[TIME *turns and faces the audience as lights shift on the gathered people.*]

NO. NO. NO.

[*During* TIME'*s final "No,"* MINA *appears from out of the "painting."*]

MINA: Hi.

MELISSA: Hi. Is it really you?

TIME AND ALL [*singing*]: NO . . .

MINA: Yeah, it's really me.

MELISSA: Are you here to stay?

TIME AND ALL [*singing*]: NO . . .

MINA: Enough questions. Time is [*after a glance at* TIME] short.

MELISSA: But—Mom—

MINA: Just tell me about your life, my beautiful girl. I want to hear all about it.

TIME AND ALL [*with a slow, sweeping feeling*]: CAN EVERYTHING BE PERFECTLY STILL?

[*The family embraces. Lights shift to focus on* TIME.]

TIME: NO.

[*Blackout.*]

ORANGE FLOWER WATER

It is the future generation that presses into being by means of these exuberant feelings and supersensible soap bubbles of ours.
—Schopenhauer

PRODUCTION HISTORY

Orange Flower Water was produced at the Contemporary American Theater Festival (Ed Herendeen, founder and producing director; Catherine Irwin, managing director; David Wanger, assistant managing director) in Shepherdstown, West Virginia, in July 2002. It was directed by Leah C. Gardiner; the set design was by Marius Henry; the lighting design was by Paul Whiteshaw; the sound design was by Kevin Lloyd; the costume design was by Daniel Urkle; the stage manager was Allison C. Wolooka; and the assistant stage manager was Danny Huernzal. The cast was as follows:

Cathy Calhoun	Mercedes Herrero
David Calhoun	Jason Field
Beth Youngquist	Libby West
Brad Youngquist	Paul Sparks

Orange Flower Water was produced at The Jungle Theater in Minneapolis, Minnesota, in July 2002. It was directed by Bain Boehlke; the set design was by Bain Boehlke; the lighting design was by Barry Browning; the composer and sound designer was Victor Zupanc; the costume design was by Amelia Cheever; the production manager was Barry Browning; and the stage manager was Elizabeth R. MacNally. The cast was as follows:

Cathy Calhoun	Amy McDonald
David Calhoun	Brian Goranson
Beth Youngquist	Jennifer Blagen
Brad Youngquist	Terry Hempleman

Orange Flower Water had its New York premiere by the Edge Theater Company at Theater for the New City in February and May 2005. It was directed by Carolyn Cantor; the set design was by David Korins; the lighting design was by Ben Stanton; original music and sound design were by Eric Shim; the costume design was by Jenny Mannis; the production stage manager was Jeff Meyers. The cast was as follows:

Cathy Calhoun	Pamela J. Gray
David Calhoun	Jason Butler Harner
Beth Youngquist	Arija Bareikis
Brad Youngquist	Paul Sparks

CHARACTERS

Cathy, *wife of David; a choir director, thirties to forties*
David, *a pharmacist, thirties to forties*
Beth, *wife of Brad, thirties to forties*
Brad, *owner of video rental stores, thirties to forties*

SCENE

The time is the present. The play takes place in various locales in Pine City, a small town in north-central Minnesota. The set is a bed and bedside table and four chairs (at the edge of the playing space) on an otherwise bare stage. On the bedside table, there is a telephone and, throughout the entire play, a small stuffed orange tiger—ideally, a "Beanie Baby."

PERFORMANCE NOTES

The four chairs onstage are for the four actors, and all the actors should be onstage and visible throughout the play.

During the preset, at the top of the show, the stage should be dimly lit, with a gentle pool of light on the stuffed tiger. Once the show begins, no more special attention needs to be paid to it.

SCENE 1

[*Music rises in the darkness. Light rises on* CATHY.]

CATHY: Dear David. Get ready. All three of the kids need to take lunches to school today. I have already made the sandwiches, but the rest needs to be assembled by yours truly. To make matters worse, Gus has early-morning math today, as well, so you have to get him there by 7:30, come back and get the girls, and take them later. And try not to fight with Ruthie. If you wake her up early enough, it should all work out, and what I have found works with her is to let her choose the radio station in the car and then shut up. Annie has Brownies after school. As for dinner: you'll be pleased to know I have reached a new state of self-awareness and have not pre-pared anything, confident that you will be taking the children out for din-ner tonight regardless of what the checkbook looks like. Have fun! Don't forget Gus has a soccer game on Saturday, and Annie is going to Taylor's birthday party. Maybe you could take Ruthie to a movie? (Can you tell I'm concerned about you two?) Finally, and don't ask me why, the painters are coming on Sunday morning, and the fumes are not good for the kids, so either go to church—ha ha—or take them out somewhere. I should be home by 5:00 P.M. Sunday afternoon. Please pick me up in the north park-ing lot of the school. The buses will all be in the south parking lot, but I need to go through the building to divest myself of all the accumulated crap these stupid choir festivals send you home with, so I'll come out the back door and wait for you there. Wish me luck! Cathy. P.S. I stood at the end of the bed this morning, once I was all dressed and ready to go, and the light was angling in from the hall, and you looked very sweet and innocent, very much the same young man who so charmingly and insinu-atingly complimented my "nice music" so many years ago. I know we get very busy around here serving the three little Hitlers, but please know, if anything should happen to me this weekend, if for some strange reason the bus drops through the bridge in Little Falls, or if I'm crushed to death by a mob of anxious sopranos, please know that I love you and feel ever so lucky and proud to be your wife in this strange and way-too-busy world we have procreated ourselves into. Yours more truly than truly can ever say . . . Cathy.

[CATHY *exits the playing area and sits down.*]

SCENE 2

[DAVID *and* BETH *rise and enter the playing area.* BETH *lies on the bed and closes her eyes.* DAVID *lies beside her and gently caresses her face.*]

DAVID: Now, I want you to put all thoughts of this world out of your mind.
BETH: David . . .
DAVID [*gently*]: Come on. "All thoughts of this world out of my mind."

[*Beat.*]

BETH: All thoughts of this world out of my mind.
DAVID: These four walls. The picturesque Holiday Haven Motel. The cars outside in the parking lot. Highway 59. It's all . . . pixilating, like little dots on a computer screen, it's all pixilating and slowly dissolving away . . .

[BETH *opens her eyes to look at him.*]

Shut your eyes.
BETH: But I think it's kinda cute the way you're, doing, you're . . . you're like a little gnome, making a spell.
DAVID: Thank you, that's my gnomish intent. Shut your eyes.
BETH: OK.

[*He waves a hand over her eyes, and she closes them; he kisses her eyelids and then continues with his spell.*]

DAVID [*quietly hypnotic*]: And now the whole town of Pine City—Lake Melissa, Sundberg's Café, the Sandwich Hut, the Voyageur—is all falling, falling through the clouds, dropping down through miles of clouds until you can't even see it anymore, Beth, it's a speck, and then it's not even a speck, it's gone. Good-bye, Pine City.

[*Beat.*]

BETH: So where are we?
DAVID: We're in a bay in a kingdom in the clouds, and it's clear and it's quiet and it's beautiful . . . and it's *just us.*
BETH: I like that.
DAVID: And in the distance . . .

[*He begins to unbutton her blouse very slowly. She opens her eyes.*]

BETH [*coy*]: What are you doing?
DAVID: In the distance—

BETH [*coy*]: I see what you're doing . . .

DAVID: In the distance, we can see huge apples . . .

BETH: Apples?

DAVID: Yes, apples . . .

[*He opens her bra, revealing her breasts.*]

Apples as high as . . . buildings, apples like two tall ships, floating on the water, golden and then shading into pink near the tops, and the sunlight and the mist, it's all like music, like the sweetest, quietest music, and we're there, and it's all . . . it's all safe . . . and quiet . . . and cool.

BETH: I'm so sick of this hot summer.

DAVID: Me too.

[*He kisses her breasts.*]

BETH: I finally got fed up the other day and bought a room air conditioner for the family room, it felt so extravagant, but—

DAVID: No, you deserve it—

BETH: They were on sale—

DAVID: Even if they weren't. Even if they weren't.

[*Brief pause as he kisses her breasts. Then the conversation continues with intermittent kissing.*]

BETH: Tell me something.

DAVID: What?

BETH: Do you really love me as much as you *think* you do?

DAVID: I *think* so.

BETH: It doesn't seem possible.

DAVID: I don't think real love ever seems possible; it just is.

BETH: I'm serious, I worry sometimes . . .

DAVID: Beth . . . listen—

BETH: What?

DAVID: I don't know what's possible or impossible . . .

BETH: I know.

DAVID: I'm *totally* out of touch with reality . . .

BETH: I know.

DAVID: All I know is when I'm with you, I feel alive, I feel like the real history of my real life is really happening; and like I'm so lucky to be able to kiss you . . . and touch you . . . and be with you and be your partner, a little while . . . on the way . . . you know?

[*He reaches behind her to unzip her skirt.*]

BETH: Wait a minute.

DAVID: What? What do you want? Wine? [*Insinuatingly, as a joke, knowing it's
stupid*] Maple syrup? You wanna be my little hotcake?

BETH: It's not . . .

DAVID: What? What is it?

BETH: Nothing.

[*Brief pause.*]

DAVID: Oh shit.

[*Long pause.*]

Beth, there is no God.

BETH: But what if there is?

DAVID: There isn't.

BETH: How do you know?

DAVID: Because.

BETH: Because why?

DAVID: Because if there was a God, Beth, come on, if, if there was a God,
then the, uh, the Crusades wouldn't have been allowed to happen; and the,
uh, Holocaust wouldn't have been allowed to happen. This whole world of
shittiness wouldn't have ever been allowed to happen if anyone who really
cared was watching.

BETH [*overlapping*]: I know what you're saying—

DAVID [*overlapping*]:—and we suffer and He just sits there and judges?

BETH: I just can't be as sure as you about everything—

DAVID: I *know*—

BETH: And you weren't raised in the church and I was, and you have to—

DAVID: I *know* that—

BETH: And I know you think that's stupid—

DAVID: I *don't* think it's stupid—

BETH: I just can't be as sure.

[*She pulls her shirt closed, crosses her arms, and sits there. Long pause.*]

DAVID: OK, so let me get this straight.

BETH: What?

DAVID [*trying to make her laugh*]: I'm sorry, I just need to understand what's
happening to me right now because my penis is kind of asking me a lot

of questions. Three years of being friends, standing next to each other at soccer games; three years of slowly realizing we're married to the wrong people—

BETH: Don't say that.

DAVID [*with firmer conviction*]: Three years of getting sicker and sicker, vomiting in our hearts from not being with each other, so you're calling me up in tears from your cell phone in the car at midnight, "Brad did this, Brad did that, I need to see you"—

BETH: I know . . .

DAVID: And I'm so sad and confused at work I'm filling prescriptions wrong and giving old ladies diarrhea, and everybody's telling me I should go in for an MRI? After three years of that, and making out in cars and making out in bathrooms at parties, and promises, promises, promises, after three years of that I finally get you in a room with me alone, and it's God? This idea?

BETH: I'm sorry. I can't change.

DAVID: Beth, I don't want you to change.

BETH: You do, though.

DAVID: No, I . . . look.

BETH: What?

DAVID: I don't want to fight.

BETH: I don't either.

DAVID: I'm here because I'm in love with you, not to fight.

BETH: I know that.

DAVID: And I don't want to make you unhappy.

BETH: I'm not unhappy, I'm just . . .

DAVID: What?

BETH: I mean, you don't really want to do this anyway, right? You love Cathy, you love your kids . . .

DAVID: Don't tell me what I don't want to do, please—

BETH: Don't be a jerk.

DAVID: Then don't tell me what I don't want to do.

BETH: Well, you *don't, really,* do you? You love Annie and Ruthie and Gus.

DAVID: Annie and Ruthie and Gus are not any happier than I am.

BETH: David, they're the happiest kids I know.

DAVID: Not inside.

BETH: You're weird.

DAVID: No, Beth, they're very uptight. And they know, I swear, they know something isn't right, because they're like always . . . consoling me in some odd way, it's creepy.

BETH: And what about Cathy?

DAVID: Cathy . . . is a mistake that I made, and I am a mistake that *she* made—

BETH [*partially overlapping previous line*]: So am I a mistake you're making? Are you a mistake I'm making?

DAVID [*rushing, overlapping*]: I don't love Cathy anymore, Beth, I love *you*. I can't help it.

BETH: And what happens when you don't love *me* anymore?

DAVID: Beth, what do you want me to do? How horrible do I have to feel? Do I wish it was different? Yes. Do I wish I didn't have to make other people miserable in order to follow my heart? Yes. But I can't help how I feel. I love you, I love you more than anything I've ever loved in my life.

BETH: Really?

DAVID: Really. I want—

BETH: Really really?

DAVID: Yes.

BETH: I mean, because, if there was ever a time when you have to be honest with me and yourself, David, it's now—

DAVID: I'm being honest with myself, I want to be with you all the time. My life is so much better when I'm with you, I don't know how to do without you the rest of the time.

BETH: You know what? You're in love with being in love, I think.

DAVID: Oh, does that thought comfort you? Does that make it easier for you to not give in and do this?

BETH: No, it doesn't—

DAVID: Look, I'm sorry I have dreams, I'm sorry I wish life was different—

BETH: You're not the only one—

DAVID [*simply, without too much anger*]: Well, you're talking like I'm the only one, "you're in love with being in love" . . .

BETH: I have dreams too!

DAVID [*knowing he's going too far as he says it*]: Well, you don't act that way.*

BETH: David, I'm scared of how big my dreams are and how much they make me feel, and *that's* why, OK, I'm sitting here trying not to do the wrong thing for any of us, OK?

DAVID: It's not your job to keep me out of hell, or keep me safe or something—

BETH: David, I just don't want to lose you as a friend.

DAVID: You won't. You'll never ever ever lose me as a friend.

BETH [*referring to **]: I don't *believe* you said that.

DAVID: What?

BETH: No.

DAVID: Tell me. Come on. Come on, I'm sorry. Forget it. I'm sorry. Just say what you want to say. Please. Just say what you want to say.

BETH: Every night I lie in bed next to Brad, you know, and I think about *us*. Every night. Even when I don't want to, when it would be easier to just forget, these thoughts come to me from somewhere underneath everything. I think about you and me and . . .

DAVID: And what?

BETH: You're gonna think this is stupid.

DAVID: You think about a baby.

BETH: Yes.

DAVID: I think about a baby too sometimes.

BETH: You do?

DAVID: Yes.

BETH: Why didn't you tell me?

DAVID: I didn't want to seem like . . .

BETH: Like what?

DAVID: Like I wanted you for . . . having my babies or something. I figured you had enough kids . . .

BETH: You should have told me.

DAVID: Yeah?

BETH: Yeah, I wouldn't have minded hearing that.

DAVID: Sorry. I think about our baby.

BETH: Me too.

[*They kiss a moment, tenderly.*]

Last night, I was thinking . . . you and I and Lily . . .

DAVID: Lily?

BETH: That's her name, in my head. Lily.

DAVID: Lily.

BETH: Yeah. Lily. She was, like, four years old, with long dark hair and really serious eyes and smart? And we went to the store at Christmastime to get stuff to make cookies—

DAVID: You?

BETH: I know, I can cook, it's a dream! But we all went to the store and it was snowing, those big fat fluffy flakes . . . dream flakes . . . and we got stuff to make sugar cookies, and on the way home, she was in her car seat and she reached in the bag and pulled out a little plastic bottle of orange flower water? Which I've read about in *Gourmet*, you know, but never seen? And she ended up spilling this orange flower water stuff all over the backseat.

And you and I had to roll down the windows, the scent was so strong . . . and the . . .

[*Brief pause.*]

DAVID: What?

BETH [*full of longing*]: And the scent of the orangey air and the coolness rushing into the car and you and me happy and Lily in the back . . . giggling . . . we were *so* happy. We were so happy. And that's just *one* night of lying there thinking in that bed. I do that *every* night. Every night for the past three years. So don't tell me I don't have dreams, OK?

DAVID: I'm sorry.

BETH: I have dreams. What I don't know is whether us taking this forward is gonna make any of them come true, or if it's just gonna make you hate me and I'll lose you as a friend, and then that'll make everything worse.

[*She clasps her bra, buttons her blouse, and swings around to sit on the edge of the bed.*]

DAVID: How could it be worse? You're married to, like, the fucking most—

BETH: David, don't talk about Brad.

DAVID: I'm sorry, that thing you told me the other day, where he was so concerned that you should keep the kids quiet while he watches the *game*?

BETH: He's not easy to live with, I know! And he takes his work very seriously—

DAVID: Oh come on, videos? And I suppose he "needs his time"?

BETH: He does!

DAVID: You've got to be kidding me. "Keep the kids quiet while I watch the fucking game"? That's not good, Beth. That's, like, "Bad Father." That's, like, one step short of *The Shining*.

[*By now,* BETH *has slipped on her shoes and is standing up.*]

BETH [*like a bullet*]: David, do you really want to be one of *them*? You think you could really take being one of *them*?

[*She points outside, i.e., toward the audience.*]

You spent all that time trying to convince me the world out there had disappeared. Why? Because it's full of people who do *this*, David. It's full of people who shit all over each other and whose word doesn't mean anything and whose kids are so screwed up, coming home to no dad or no mom, and it's all sold to us like it's almost normal, are we really gonna be like them? Isn't that what we're asking each other to do?

DAVID [*searching for a way back to her*]: No, we're asking each other for . . . for a moment of . . . goodness . . . in a life that is mostly unpleasant and way too short—

BETH [*searching just as hard*]: But there are no moments of goodness that don't . . . come with responsibilities.

DAVID: I know that.

BETH: I don't think you do.

[*Beat.* DAVID *lies down on the bed and screams into the pillow for a good ten seconds.*]

DAVID [*into pillow*]: Aahhhhh!

[*Beat.*]

BETH: We should go.

[*Beat.*]

DAVID [*looking up from pillow*]: You know what my mistake was?

BETH: David, this is not a mistake.

DAVID: You know where I screwed this up?

BETH: David, we're doing the right thing. You have a life. I have a life. Our kids have lives. This is—

DAVID: I never should have talked. Hesitation turns everything into a discussion. And we've been hesitating ever since we met.

[*He rises.*]

I never should have *talked*.

[*He goes to her, puts his arms around her. They look at each other for a while, and then he kisses her. After a moment, she pulls away.*]

BETH: No.

DAVID [*giving up*]: OK. OK.

[*A moment passes, and then he takes the bottom of her skirt in his hands and pulls it up and pulls her tightly against him.*]

Beth, I can't make it seem right, and I can't make the world go away, and I can't even kid myself it's right. I just *want* you, OK? I want to be *with* you . . . and *for* you . . . and *in* you. Right now. OK?

[*Brief pause.*]

BETH [*almost dizzy*]: OK.

[*They kiss. Music rises.* DAVID *and* BETH *exit the bed area.* BETH *sits down in her chair.*]

SCENE 3

[BRAD *stands and meets* DAVID *in a sunny pool of light. They gaze out toward the audience, watching a soccer game.*]

BRAD: Looks like old Arshavir Blackwell's gonna score our only goal again. Christ, he must absolutely hate fucking life being on this team. [*To the field*] Go! Now take it downfield!

DAVID: Everybody feeds him the ball, that must be kinda fun for him—

BRAD: I know, but the only reason—[*To the field*] Don't be scared to get in front of him, Carl! [*To* DAVID] The only reason his parents have him playing rec soccer at all is to teach him a lesson.

DAVID: Yeah?

BRAD: Yeah, he used to be on a traveling team in the Cities, but they thought he was getting a big head. [*To the field*] Attaboy, Carl, get in his face! [*To* DAVID] So they stuck him with our kids for a season. They live in Albertville so the commute's the same either way. What the hell kinda name is that anyway, Arshavir?

DAVID: I think it's Armenian.

BRAD: If my parents had done that to me, given me a name like that, I woulda taken a shit on the dining room table every night. I woulda crapped 'em out a *great* big bowl of snakes.

[*Beat.*]

You played sports? Back in school?

DAVID: Sure. Not soccer, but I, I was on the tennis team—

BRAD [*sardonically*]: Yeah, that's a sport. Where's the little woman?

DAVID: Oh, she took, um . . . Ruthie and Annie started ballet today, so—

BRAD: That new place across from the movie theater?

DAVID: Yeah—

BRAD: I thought that's what that might be. I wasn't sure, looking in.

DAVID: Yeah, it's a ballet studio.

BRAD: You seen that babe who runs it then?

DAVID: Mm-hmm.

BRAD: Would *you?*

DAVID: Oh sure. Totally.

BRAD: I saw her in there painting the other night, a couple months ago, I guess it was, but she was hot. She had on a leotard and all that long black hair. And she's single?

DAVID: I think so, yeah. But I think she might be the girlfriend of that new guy at the radio station, Wigdahl whatever, but—

BRAD: OK, tell me something.

DAVID: OK.

BRAD [*after much thought*]: Her or . . .

[*He points to a woman nearby.*]

Katie Amundson. Desert island, which one do you take?

DAVID [*a little uneasy*]: I don't know . . . you tell—

BRAD: Come on, have a fucking conversation with me, which one? [*To the field*] Hand ball! Ref! Ref! That was a hand ball! [*To* DAVID] Which one? [*To the field*] Carl, don't let him get behind you like that!

DAVID: Katie.

BRAD: Yeah, I know, I know, for one night, the other maybe, but—you're right—it's very deceptive—[*To the field*] Don't be afraid to get hurt, Carl! You can't play afraid! [*To* DAVID] So. Katie.

DAVID: Yeah. She's got something.

BRAD: I'll tell you what she's got, she's got that ass. She's got that undeniable ass. [*To the field*] Hey, Gus, nice D! [*To* DAVID] Did you see that?

DAVID: Yeah. [*To the field*] Way to go, Gussie!

BRAD: He's a good kid.

DAVID: Thanks.

BRAD: OK. Katie Amundson or . . .

[*He surreptitiously points to another woman nearby.*]

DAVID: Elena?

BRAD: Yeah.

DAVID: Are you serious?

BRAD: You getting picky?

DAVID: No, it's just . . .

BRAD: See, I *like* that eye.

DAVID: It would drive me crazy, I think—

BRAD: If it went *out*, yeah, like a walleye, yeah, but *in* a little like that's kinda sweet. It's kinda helpless-looking, like you could catch her, you know? Like she'd be at the back of the herd, dawdling.

[BRAD *crosses his eyes.*]

DAVID: No.

BRAD [*still with eyes crossed*]: You don't see any charm in this at all?

DAVID: No.

BRAD: See, I'm taking Elena on that one. Does Katie know you feel this way about her?

DAVID: No.

BRAD: You want me to get her over here and you two could set up some time maybe?

DAVID: No. Thanks.

BRAD: Cathy'd bite your balls off, wouldn't she?

DAVID: Oh yeah.

BRAD: So what about Beth? [*To field*] Go! Go! Go! Go!

DAVID: Your Beth?

BRAD: Yeah. My Beth. Katie or my Beth?

DAVID [*bewildered*]: I don't know, what about Cathy?

BRAD: Cathy or Katie?

DAVID: Yeah.

BRAD: For me?

DAVID: Yeah.

BRAD: That's easy, I'll take Cathy. [*Immediately, to the field, clapping*] Good game, you guys! Good game! Way to hustle out there! Good hustle, Arshavir! Good hustle, Carl! [*To DAVID*] Wouldn't you take Beth?

DAVID: Over Katie?

BRAD: Over Cathy. [*To the field*] Nice game, Gus! Carl, get your stuff together!

DAVID: Uhh . . .

BRAD: I'll see you next weekend and hey, by the way, Beth told me to ask you, she knows her insurance won't let her refill her pills until the end of the month, but Oscar got into her purse and ate 'em . . . ?

DAVID: Is he OK?

BRAD: He doesn't seem any sicker than usual. He ate her lipstick and blush and everything.

DAVID: Christ.

BRAD: Yeah, he eats her old tampons if she doesn't cover the bathroom trash tight enough. [*With too much edge*] It's fucking disgusting.

[BRAD *puts out his hand to shake.*]

Nice talking to you, I'll see you next week.

[*They shake hands. As* BRAD *exits, he calls upstage, in a joking sotto voce* . . .]

Hey, Katie, I think David over here wants a word with you! No, I'm just kidding, bye!

[*He exits to his chair, followed by a disconcerted* DAVID. *Music rises.* DAVID *sits down.*]

SCENE 4

[BETH *stands, goes to the bed area and pulls a suitcase out from under the bed, sets it on the bed, and opens it. She removes several articles of clothing and sets them beside the suitcase on the bed. She changes blouses. Meanwhile,* BRAD *has put on an apron that says "World's Greatest Dad," and he enters the scene carrying a large spatula and a container of charcoal lighter fluid as* BETH *begins putting the clothes carefully back into the suitcase.*]

BRAD: Have you seen the other one of these?
BETH: No.
BRAD: I thought I asked you to buy two, we're always running out—
BETH: Gosh—
BRAD: This one's hardly got enough to—
BETH [*tense and falsely*]: Gosh, honey, I'm sorry, I must not have gotten around to it.
BRAD: What are you doing? What are you doing?
BETH: What does it look like I'm doing, Brad? I'm leaving.
BRAD: What?
BETH: You heard me, I'm leaving.
BRAD [*gesturing to where he entered*]: Because of that down there? Because—
BETH: I'm not stupid, Brad!
BRAD: No, this is funny . . .
BETH: The boys aren't stupid and I'm not stupid, and to say something like that—

BRAD: I didn't mean you were stupid, it was just a . . . comment, for Christ's sake—

BETH: In front of *my* friends.

BRAD: Beth, they know—

BETH: That you think you can say something like that is so scary to me—

BRAD: Beth, they know I'm a prick, they don't listen to what I say.

BETH: They know you're a prick.

BRAD: Yeah, everybody knows I'm a prick!

BETH: And you're able to live with that?

BRAD: It's who I am! Look, I'm sorry, I—I say things! I don't mean them, I just say them! You know that!

BETH: No, what I know is . . . I'm really not happy . . . and I haven't been happy for a long time, and that's . . . just . . . I gotta go.

[*She closes the suitcase.*]

I gotta go.

BRAD: No.

BETH: What does that mean?

BRAD: It means no, I won't let you go. You can't—

BETH: Do you want me to scream? Do you want to make a big scene with Denny and Sonya downstairs?

BRAD: Go ahead.

BETH: Brad!

BRAD: Denny and Sonya can go fuck themselves for all I care, my wife isn't walking out the door!

BETH: Like I'm some character in a story!

BRAD: What the hell does—

BETH: You say it like I'm some little character in a story, "My wife's not gonna . . ." *I'm not some little character in a story!*

[*As she picks up the suitcase and attempts to exit past him, he touches her. She drops the suitcase and screams at the top of her lungs.*]

DON'T TOUCH ME! DON'T TOUCH ME!

[*He backs off.*]

BRAD: Sorry!

BETH: Every time you touch me, it's like being raped!

BRAD: Jesus Christ, you're a fucking freak!

BETH: No, I'm not.

BRAD: Just tell me where you're going.

BETH: No! It's none of your business!

BRAD: You're gonna run to what's his name, your little boyfriend?

BETH: I'm going to the cabin, you don't know what—

BRAD: You're gonna go run to your little fucking boyfriend.

BETH: I don't know what you're talking about.

BRAD: Oh, fuck you!

BETH: No, you think I need someone to run to, like I need somebody, like living in the same house with you for fifteen years isn't enough to make me sick to my stomach? I don't need another reason to be miserable, Brad! You're all the reason anyone would ever need!

BRAD: Beth, I know you and that pharmacist have been fucking around behind my back. I wasn't gonna do anything about it—

BETH [*overlapping*]: You are so wrong about—

BRAD [*overlapping*]:—because I didn't want the boys to find out their mother was a whore!

[*She picks up the suitcase.*]

BETH: You know what, I'm going. You obviously have some idea in your head that is totally of your own creation and—

[*He reaches to stop her.*]

[*Like an animal*] I SAID DON'T TOUCH ME!

[*She starts to go.*]

BRAD [*a little unnerved*]: So, so, so right in front of Denny and Sonya . . .

BETH: Everyone knows you're a prick, Brad! I'm sure they'll take it in stride!

BRAD: He won't leave Cathy, you know that, don't you?

BETH: I'm not even gonna have this discussion because, you know what? I don't know what it's about!

BRAD: He won't!

BETH [*suddenly shifting*]: Look, he knows what he wants and I know what I want and we've been very clear with each other—

BRAD: Aha! So you *are* fucking this guy!

BETH: Yeah, Brad, I guess I am, I'm "fucking this guy"!

BRAD: Oh, maybe I shouldn't use such bad language, you're right. It's such a beautiful thing when two people who are married to other people can put their stinky little parts in each other, I'm sorry if I made it sound cheap! Fuckin' A!

BETH: I know it's cheap.

BRAD: Oh, you do?

BETH: Yes, I *know* it's not good—

BRAD: But you *don't* know there's no way he's leaving those three little kids? Come on! You've gotta know *that*, right? He's never gonna leave those kids. That bitch wife of his has him wound around her finger tighter than a Duncan fucking yo-yo. Have you ever seen him with her at the store picking out movies? It's Merchant Ivory, Jane Austen, Merchant Ivory, Jane Austen, English every single fucking time, he's not going *anywhere*! You *must* know that, Beth. You're not stupid, you *must*.

[*Beat.*]

So look, let's go downstairs and have a beer and—

BETH: No!

BRAD: Come on, you can bitch to Sonya, Denny, and I'll take the boys to the lake for a swim or something—

BETH: NO!

BRAD: Do you want me to just send 'em home?

BETH: No. I don't know!

BRAD: Look, let me go down there and tell 'em we need a little time—

BETH: No!

BRAD: Yes, I'll let them get the coals started, maybe Denny can figure out how to use that thing of yours where it works without fluid and we'll . . . I'll be right back up.

[*Brief pause.*]

BETH [*resignedly*]: Whatever.

[BRAD *exits and sits in his chair.* BETH *carries the suitcase back into the room and sets it down. She sits on the edge of the bed and bursts into tears. She cries for a minute or two then stands and looks around the room at all the things she'll be leaving. Note: this whole sequence should take longer than is normal—for a play—or comfortable. Then, finally,* BRAD *rises and enters the scene again, having taken off his apron.*]

BRAD: They decided to go home.

BETH: I'm sorry. I'll call Sonya later and explain—

BRAD: No, they understand, it's not a big deal.

BETH: It's a big deal, Brad.

BRAD: You know what I mean.

BETH: What did you tell them?

BRAD: I said you're fucking the pharmacist at Sundberg's and we gotta talk.

BETH: You did not.

BRAD: No, I didn't, I just said we had to talk, that's all. And they took the boys.

BETH: Where?

BRAD: I don't know, they'll go to Perkins or somewhere and have some dinner, I guess.

[*Brief pause.*]

BETH: God.

BRAD: What?

BETH: Everything actually has to happen, doesn't it? You think in your mind things can happen without happening, but in the end, they always have to actually happen. Actual kids have to get driven away by actual friends . . . and actual people have to sit there and actually . . . live.

[*Brief pause.*]

BRAD: So you know for a fact he's leaving Cathy?

BETH [*beaten down*]: God, I don't know, Brad. And I don't care, we're . . . this is not about that. That's as much of a mistake probably as this was, I'm the queen of romantic mistakes—

BRAD: You and me.

BETH: What?

BRAD: A mistake?

BETH: Yeah!

BRAD: It wasn't a mistake for me.

BETH: What am I supposed to say to that?

BRAD: Nothing, but that's . . .

BETH: All of a sudden you have feelings . . . ?

BRAD [*honest*]: No, it's just what I'm saying. Is it perfect all the time? No way. But it's not a mistake. But you, you really think—

BETH: Look . . . do you really want to have this conversation? Because, truthfully, I just want to go.

BRAD: Then go! Fuck it!

[*He screams fiercely, right in her face.*]

Go! Go! Go! Go!

BETH [*overlapping*]: Don't you understand, you stupid idiot, this doesn't make me happy?

BRAD [*overlapping*]: Go! Go! GO! GO! GO!

BETH: Don't you understand that? If I felt like I had a choice, I'd . . . I'd have one!

[*A pause. He steps away from her. After a moment,* BETH *rises.*]

BRAD [*still angry*]: You're going up to the cabin?

BETH: Yeah.

BRAD: Is he gonna be up there?

BETH: No.

BRAD: *Yes.*

BETH: I don't know! Does it matter?

BRAD: Yes, it's my fucking cabin! I built it! I don't want some shit-for-brains pharmacist fucking my wife in that cabin!

BETH: Then he won't come up!

BRAD: I'm just asking for the common courtesy of not having him spray *his* come all over *my* pillow!

BETH: I said he won't come up, shut up about it already! I wasn't planning on it anyway, but—

BRAD: Thank you!

BETH: God! You're such a pig!

BRAD: Does Cathy know?

BETH: *I don't know!* I told you, that's not what this is about! This is you and me, Brad! David or no David—

BRAD: Fuck, don't you say that name in my house . . .

BETH: David or no David—

BRAD: *Don't say that motherfucker's name in this house, Beth!*

BETH: He doesn't know what I'm doing, I haven't told him about this. It's not like we're on walkie-talkies all the time, it's not that serious.

BRAD: So you don't know if Cathy knows?

BETH: No, I don't, and I don't care.

BRAD: Because the minute you walk out the door, I'm gonna call over there and tell her her husband is fucking my wife.

BETH: Is that supposed to make me stay? You want me to stay with you for his sake?

BRAD: I don't know, Beth! You're the one who said this shit has to actually happen! All I'm saying is, walk out the door and things will start to actually fucking happen!

BETH: And you have to hurt everybody else?

BRAD: Yeah, I do!

BETH: This is not about them!

BRAD: Bullshit! Bull-fat-fucking-bull-*shit*! We were happy—

BETH: We were never happy, Brad, like people are supposed to be—

BRAD: Bullshit! We were happy for fifteen years—

BETH: I was never happy!

BRAD: Is that what he tells you, that you've never been happy?

BETH: No!

BRAD: This *wonderful* guy—

BETH: It's the *truth*!

BRAD: He takes half your fucking life and pisses all over it just so he can get in your pants, getting you to believe you've never been happy? We've fucked in this bed, shit, how many times, Beth? A thousand times? Two thousand times? And you're fuckin' telling me you've never been happy? What, that you fuckin' faked it *every* time? Just tell me you faked it every time! Every time you said you loved me, every time you pushed that pussy of yours in my face and said you loved me—

BETH: There's more to life than sex, you *idiot*!

BRAD [*a sudden rush, a new thought*]: And you *owe* me nothing?

BETH: What?

BRAD: I made a promise to you and I've kept it all these years and you owe me *nothing*?

BETH: I've cleaned your house and fed you and fed your kids and made sure everything—

BRAD: I'm talking about a *promise*—

BETH: If anything, you owe *me*—

BRAD: I'm not talking about housework, I'm talking about a *promise*! I took my life, I could have done whatever I wanted to with it, but I chased you down—stupid fucking me—and you never let me forget that—"oh, he had to chase me down"—"I wasn't really ready, but he was *so persistent*"—and stupid me, I chased you down because I thought you were the most beautiful woman I'd ever seen in my life and I thought, "Shit, Brad, you *are* an idiot, but maybe, just maybe, she'll see something in you that you don't even see, you know?"

BETH: I know, I'm the worst thing that ever happened to you, I know that!

BRAD: *Nobody*, none of my friends thought you'd go out with me, I remember Slick said it was a "logical impossibility"—

BETH: And it still is, that's the problem!

BRAD: So why did you say yes? You bitch! Why did we have kids? Why did you waste my time for the past fifteen motherfucking years?

BETH: Because I didn't know what else to do! And I didn't think I would ever be good at anything! And I didn't think it would last this long!

BRAD: Oh, should I have died? Did I miss my cue?

BETH: No, it's just . . . *life gets long sometimes!*

BRAD: You know, you're full of shit!

BETH: I am not full of shit, Brad, I'm just tired of being married to you, and that's all it is! It's nothing as complicated as you seem to want to make it.

BRAD: You loved me!

BETH: I didn't love you, I was scared to live!

BRAD: No, you loved me, you did! And when this whole thing turns to shit on you, you're gonna know that too, in the pit of your fucking heart, you're gonna know it like you never knew anything!

[*He picks up the phone.*]

What's his number?

BETH: Don't call him.

BRAD: What's his fucking number?

BETH: Brad, if you wanna be mad at somebody, be mad at me!

[*She tries to hang up the phone.*]

BRAD: Don't touch that fucking phone again!

BETH: Look, you want me to stay, I'll stay, but—

[*Again, she tries to hang up the phone.*]

BRAD: I said, don't touch this fucking phone!

[*He pushes her away.*]

You think it feels like being raped every time I touch you? I'll throw you down and fuck you right now, you fucking cunt!

BETH: I'm leaving. Before you do something that gets you locked up in prison. Because that wouldn't be good for the boys.

[*She picks up the suitcase.*]

BRAD [*yelling*]: Oh, do us all a favor!

BETH: I am!

BRAD [*yelling*]: Save me from *myself*! What a fucking joke!

BETH: You can stop yelling, Brad, I'm leaving!

BRAD [*top of his lungs*]: Go ahead! And I'll tell the boys when they get back all about their mother the fucking whore!

[BETH *goes upstage and sits down in her chair.* BRAD *yells in her direction even louder, so all the neighbors can hear.*]

I oughta screw you right through this bed and straight down to hell where you came from, you fucking cunt! You motherfucking cunt!

[*Music rises. He dials the phone, waits.*]

[*Still rattled, his voice hoarse*] Hi, Audrey. Pull up David Calhoun on the computer. What's his number? Thanks.

[*He waits. He hangs up. He dials. He waits.*]

Hi, is this Cathy? Yeah, this is Brad Youngquist. Yeah, from the video store. No, I know, there's, it's not overdue yet, listen, I just thought you should know your husband's fucking my wife.

[*He slams down the phone, sits on the bed. Lights shift as music rises.*]

SCENE 5

[*After a brief pause,* BRAD *rises slowly from the bed and moves into a pool of light downstage.*]

BRAD: Dear Beth. The boys are staying at Denny and Sonya's tonight, the house is a mess, and I'm a little drunk. ("No, you're a big drunk," I can hear you say in my mind.) As you of all people know, I'm not very good with words. And I know I'm not easy to live with. But I hope you'll give me another chance. I'm willing to put all of this shit behind us if you'll give me another chance. I want another chance. I need another chance. You're the best thing that has ever happened to me in my life, and I can't believe I'm sitting here on the edge of losing you forever. If you're really happier with the pharmacist, then I guess you should be with him, but I really hope that after a few days up there at Chez Youngquist, you'll want to come home to me. I'll build you your own bathroom up there, if you want. I love you, Beth. I'm not perfect, but I do love you the best I know how, and I can learn and change and be better, if you'll just come home. You are so pretty. Looking around right now, I see you are the pretty part of everything here.

Without you here, this place is really a dump. And I don't mean cleaning-wise. You know what I mean. Please come home if you want to and we will be lovers again. From the bottom of an ocean of that awful beer your brother makes and which I finally got desperate enough to take a crack at . . . your biggest fan . . . Brad.

[BRAD *exits and sits down in his seat. Music continues.*]

SCENE 6

[DAVID *and* CATHY *are on the bed. The atmosphere is one of grim, slightly absurd resignation. Note: this entire scene should be done quietly enough to indicate that neither participant wishes to wake the children.*]

CATHY: I'm not going to tell the kids for you.
DAVID: I wouldn't ask you to.
CATHY: Oh, I think you would. I think you were just about to.
DAVID: I wasn't.
CATHY: It's going to seriously mess up Gus.
DAVID: I'll work it out with him.
CATHY: The girls I can handle, I can train them not to hate men—I would have had to do that anyway—but Gus, I don't have access to him.
DAVID: I don't either, really—
CATHY: *That's* an excuse.
DAVID: Look, I said I'll talk to him! I'll talk to them in the morning.
CATHY: Then I'll leave the house, because I don't think I can take it.
DAVID: Look, do you want me to go?
CATHY: No.

[*Long pause.*]

You know what I want?
DAVID: What?
CATHY: You want to do what I want? You want to console me? Make yourself feel better?
DAVID: What?

[*She crawls on top of him, clearly trying to initiate sex. Brief pause.*]

I can't.
CATHY: Why? Because you don't "love" me anymore? Your license to say shit like that has been permanently revoked.

DAVID: Cathy, this won't stop me from leaving.

CATHY: Oh, stop being so vain. Did it ever occur to you that maybe I'm glad to be rid of you? You're such a shit to the kids lately anyway, David, it's probably all for the best.

DAVID: Honey, I think you're a little confused.

[*She slaps his face hard.*]

CATHY: No. I'm not. I know exactly what I'm doing. OK?

DAVID: OK.

[*Straddling him, she begins slowly moving her hips up and down. Just a little.*]

CATHY: Give me your hands.

DAVID: No.

CATHY: Come on, hold me up a little.

[*After a moment, he offers his hands. They link hands.*]

DAVID: I can't get it up. I won't. I can't.

CATHY: You're so noble. It's touching. Let's get Beth on the phone and tell her how you're enduring this trial so gallantly by refusing to get an erection.

DAVID: This really doesn't seem like you.

CATHY: David, you're so self-involved, I don't think you really know what seems like me or doesn't seem like me anymore.

DAVID: You might be right.

CATHY: Hold me around the back.

DAVID: No! Just . . . get off me . . .

CATHY: David, if you want to go stay somewhere else, then do it, but if you're gonna stay here, then . . .

DAVID: What?

[*A long beat.*]

CATHY: Get on the team!

DAVID: "Get on the team."

CATHY: Yes! Get on the team . . . you jerk.

[*Brief pause. He laughs a little, she laughs back, and he relents, puts his hands on her behind, beneath her nightgown. She continues moving above him. After a while, she leans down and kisses him. He does not respond. She begins kissing his face, shoulders, and chest every now and then.*]

How is it with Beth?

DAVID: What?

CATHY: The sex.

DAVID: You don't want to know.

CATHY: Yes, I do.

DAVID: It's great.

CATHY: It's easy for it to be great when you don't have to watch the person pee every morning.

DAVID: So I should wake up and realize Beth won't do it for me once I've got her all to myself, twenty-four hours a day.

CATHY: That, and the self-hatred for what you've done to the kids. And Brad showing up every morning to take a shit on your porch.

DAVID: Did he tell you that?

CATHY: Yeah.

DAVID: That guy is fascinated with shitting on things. I think he must hold his tension in his ass, that's why he's always got prostate problems.

CATHY: And where do you hold yours?

DAVID: My tension?

CATHY: Mm-hmm.

DAVID: The obvious answer is my dick, I guess, I don't know, you obviously have a plan—

CATHY: I think you hold it in me.

DAVID: I hold *my* tension in *you*. That's a trick.

CATHY: Isn't it? See, I think, in little ways you ask me to hold it for you, and I do, and then you hate me for helping you, so you run off and generate passionate feelings for other women.

DAVID: There are no other women, it's just Beth. It's always been just Beth.

CATHY: Katie Amundson.

DAVID: Did you and Brad have dinner or something together?

CATHY: We had coffee.

DAVID: Where?

CATHY: At Sundberg's.

DAVID: You shit!

CATHY: It wasn't my idea. It was Brad's, he said he wanted to infiltrate the enemy camp.

DAVID: Right in front of everybody at Sundberg's?

CATHY: David, it's a free world! You've proved that. It's a great, big, ugly, free world.

[*Long silence. Suddenly they kiss with real abandon, tinged with anger, for the first time. After a while, she pulls back.*]

Today in class, I was handing back tests . . .

DAVID: Yeah?

CATHY: I'd given them this very simple ear training test, just for fun, and little Jason Pearson, he said, "Mrs. Calhoun? I got nine out of twenty-five. Is that good?" So I sent him down to Ed's room, I said, "Go ask your math teacher."

DAVID: You still like teaching?

CATHY: I do. It's . . . you know what it is, ultimately? I think it's as simple as I enjoy the company of kids.

[*After a moment.*]

You know who doesn't like school, though . . .

DAVID: Ruthie.

CATHY: She was complaining to me today about how all her teachers expect her to be perfect. She said, "The more I do better, the more they expect me to do better. It's too much." She said that about twenty times, staring into the rearview mirror like this total drama queen: "It's too much. It's too much."

DAVID: Are you trying to make me sentimental about the kids? It's working.

CATHY: I'm just telling you about your children, David. I'm not as cagey as you think.

DAVID: You're the smartest person *I* know.

CATHY: I am not.

DAVID: No, you know what I mean. You're smart about bullshit.

CATHY: So why do you want to be with her? You want somebody dumb?

DAVID: She's not dumb. She's just a little more naive than you.

CATHY: She'd have to be, to think you could actually love her.

DAVID: I do love her.

CATHY: Uh-huh.

DAVID: I do.

CATHY: David, can you please reach a little inside me and do your part?

[*He's nonplussed.*]

What?

DAVID: I don't know, you've never been this direct before.

CATHY: Well, our marriage is essentially over, right?

DAVID: I think so, yeah.

CATHY: You're leaving me for Beth, right, you two are gonna go be boyfriend and girlfriend?

DAVID: I hope so.

CATHY: Then do I really need to waste my dignity on you?

DAVID: OK.

[*He does something beneath her nightgown which registers a nonverbal response.*]

CATHY: Thank you.

[*A few moments without words pass.*]

I thought you said you couldn't get it up.

DAVID: Honey, this is just making me sad.

CATHY: Look, unless you want me to start screaming ... at the top of my lungs ... and have the children come running in here ... and watch you pack your bags right now, you'll shut up, OK?

[*Brief pause.*]

DAVID: OK.

[*Brief pause.*]

CATHY: I want you inside me.

[DAVID *sighs.*]

Shit, David, would you please stop pretending to care? Picture *her*. Or Katie Amundson.

DAVID: I don't have to picture anybody else.

CATHY: Don't do me any favors.

DAVID: I do think you're pretty.

CATHY [*quoting* The Rainmaker]: "You're pretty, Lizzie. You're pretty."

DAVID: Shut up!

CATHY: You shut up!

[*A moment passes. Through a silent agreement, over the course of ten seconds or so, they work together to get him inside her.*]

There. Isn't that better?

DAVID: Better than what?

CATHY: Fighting.

DAVID: It feels like fighting to me. I feel like I'm getting the shit beat out of me.

[*Brief pause. As the scene continues, the pace of their physicality accelerates slightly, their words more and more broken up by breaths and silences. This acceleration is gentle, however, and the volume is never loud enough to wake up the kids.*]

CATHY: It was actually fun . . . having coffee with Brad. He's such a palooka, he's kinda sweet.

DAVID: He's not very sweet to Beth.

CATHY: Poor her. But he's not as dumb as you think, David. He's known about you two for a long time, long before he called.

DAVID: She told him?

CATHY: No, don't worry, your little sweetie didn't betray your confidence. He just knew. He told me . . . he told me the day he figured it out, he was driving by Warehouse Foods . . . and he saw a man and a woman loading groceries into the back of a car. One was lifting them out of the cart and then handing them . . . handing them to the other one to put into the trunk. And he said it suddenly occurred to him, "I bet they think they're two different people."

DAVID: What the hell does that mean?

CATHY: That's what I said. He said for one second, it looked to him like they were really one person, but with two bodies. But one person. Connected. By invisible threads. And that's when he knew.

DAVID: Brad said this.

CATHY: Yeah.

DAVID: The video store guy.

CATHY: Yeah, I know. But what it made *me* think was . . . what I didn't tell *him* . . . what it made me think was . . . maybe we're *all* the same person. Maybe all of us . . .

[*Their lovemaking escalates.*]

DAVID: Are you OK?

CATHY: I'm OK. Are you OK?

DAVID: I'm OK.

[*After two minutes of wordless intercourse, they both have orgasms. She collapses onto him. A long time passes in silence.*]

I'll tell the kids in the morning.

[*Brief pause.*]

CATHY [*with great sadness but no tears*]: Fine.

[*After a moment or two, she begins to cry. He moves to put his arms around her. She sits up a little, still on top of him, and pushes his arms away.*]

[*Still crying*] No! I don't want any sympathy. I don't want any of your shitty little sympathy.

[*Brief pause. He wipes her tears away as they fall on his face.*]

Sorry.

[*She settles back down onto him. He does not embrace her; his arms lie stretched out impotently at his sides. A moment. Then music rises. Lights shift.*]

SCENE 7

[DAVID *and* CATHY *rise from the bed and get dressed. Once dressed,* DAVID *goes upstage to his seat.* BETH *rises, wearing a raincoat and carrying an umbrella, and meets* CATHY *downstage in a pool of gray light. Sounds of rain and periodic thunder can be heard, nothing too threatening. They are both focused on the soccer field.* CATHY *is eating candy from a small bag.*]

CATHY: That Arshavir is something else, isn't he?
BETH [*uncomfortable*]: Uh, I just thank God, for Carl's sake, he's on the team.
CATHY: Gussie, too.
BETH: He's a natural.
CATHY [*to the field*]: Get in there, Gus! Good man!

[*Brief pause. Thunderclap and the sound of intensified rain.*]

Mind if I get under there? Just for a second?
BETH: Uhh, sure.

[CATHY *gets under the umbrella next to* BETH. *Beat.*]

CATHY: You want some sour Skittles?
BETH: No, thanks.
CATHY: Gus tells me they're the biggest thing to happen to candy since Gushers. They're not bad.

[*Beat.*]

BETH: I'll try one. I've seen the commercials, I was wondering.

[CATHY *gives her some candy. They eat for a moment in silence. After a beat,* BETH *holds out her hand for some more.*]

Just, like, two.
CATHY: See what I mean?
BETH: Yeah.

[*Brief pause as they chew.*]

CATHY: So look, what am I doing over here with candy, I'll tell you, I'm the one who's gonna be taking over your Meals on Wheels route.
BETH: At First Lutheran?
CATHY: Yeah, I figure now that David's out of the house, I don't care, I'm gonna at least join a church and get 'em baptized. [*Gently facetious*] So they don't rot in hell.
BETH: Yeah, I think that's good.
CATHY: You can tell him, too, if you want—
BETH: I don't . . . whatever. You can tell him.
CATHY: Anyway, I just wanted to warn you, I'll be the one showing up at the church to get trained in, so don't freak out.
BETH: I could get someone else to do it, if you want—I mean—it's pretty much nothing—
CATHY: No, I think that's what church is for, right?
BETH: For . . . ?
CATHY: For breaking down the barriers we put up in the world? Between people?
BETH: Are you serious?
CATHY: Yeah. I mean, it should be; that's the point, right?
BETH: In theory.
CATHY: Well . . . here's a barrier.
BETH: Yes, here is one, you're right.
CATHY [*to the field*]: You have to run, Gus! You have to actually run!

[CATHY *offers* BETH *more candy.*]

More?

[BETH *takes a few.*]

BETH: Thanks.
CATHY [*to* BETH]: But you, you're quitting.

BETH: Yeah, who told you that?
CATHY [*overlapping*]: Pastor Ed.

[*Beat.*]

BETH: Why did he tell you that?
CATHY: Why are you quitting?

[*Beat.*]

BETH: Are you really asking me?
CATHY: Yeah.
BETH: This is a real conversation?
CATHY: Yeah.
BETH: And you're asking me because ...
CATHY: Because I want you to know you don't have to quit because of me and the kids, that's all. I wouldn't want that.
BETH: Wouldn't you?
CATHY: No.
BETH: I'm quitting because ...
CATHY: David's making you.
BETH: No. I'm quitting because when I try to pray now ... I feel stupid.

[*Beat.*]

CATHY: I think everybody feels that way. It's a stupid thing to do.
BETH: Do you pray?
CATHY: Sometimes. Not as much as I used to. But sometimes.
BETH [*very absently, with an eye on the soccer game*]: When I was really little, you know ... I thought God was like my dad, only bigger. And, uh, just like it felt to walk through our house where my dad had built all the furniture, that's how it felt to walk through the whole world. Everything seemed like it had a little note taped to it: "Thought you might like this tree!" "Thought you might like this sunset!" "Thought you might like this cute boy! I made him just for you!"

[BETH *looks to* CATHY, *who smiles a little.*]

And, uh, I told my guidance counselor in high school, you won't believe this, I told her I didn't need to choose a career, because God had a plan for my life? And she said she was part of how God let people *in* on His plans. And I believed her. And *that* was the beginning of the end ... because after that, it was so easy to see everything that way, right? Making out in the back of Jeff Kosternople's VW Bus seemed like God's way of letting me *in* on something; and drinking too much in college was God's way of letting me *in* on something. And now, just when I would really love to look out over those trees, Cathy, and see a little note: "Hi, Beth! Thought you might like this world"—I look around and there are no notes on anything, anywhere.

[*Beat.*]

Cathy, I'm really sorry about what's happened. If it ever felt like a choice, I'd have chosen differently, but it never did. I'm sorry.

CATHY [*abruptly*]: Are you going to keep the kids?

BETH [*a little chastened*]: Not if Brad has his way . . . his lawyer's really good, it's kinda scary—

CATHY: So it'll just be you and David?

BETH: Yeah—

CATHY: Because you should know, he's had a low sperm count the past few years.

[BETH *doesn't know what to say.*]

We were trying up until two years ago to have one more. He blamed me until we went to a doctor in the Cities and did the tests, but who knows, if he's happier with you, maybe that'll bring it back up. It works that way sometimes—

BETH: Cathy, listen—

CATHY [*plunging on, her bitterness showing through*]: —in which case, if it does, let me tell you, he's very good with babies, loves babies, but once they're no longer helpless, Beth, he blames them for everything, he can be very petty when it comes to—

BETH [*harder*]: *Cathy.*

[CATHY *stops.*]

I really don't want to have this conversation.

CATHY: Oh. OK.

[CATHY *takes a few steps away.*]

But I'll see you on Wednesday.

BETH: Yeah. I guess. I'll show you how to feed the old people.

CATHY: Beth, I hate to tell you this, but I think we *are* the old people.

[CATHY *exits upstage to her chair. Music rises. Lights shift as* BETH *enters the bedroom area and joins* DAVID *there. Lights shift.*]

SCENE 8

[DAVID *and* BETH *are standing in the bed area, both wearing light jackets.*]

BETH: It's a nice house.

DAVID: I like the trees. I killed every tree at our house within about three years of moving in. It'd be fun to have trees again.

BETH: Something to kill.

DAVID: No, I'd be better to these trees.

[*Brief pause as they look around the room.*]

BETH: It would be nice to have a few more bedrooms.

DAVID [*a little edgy*]: I know, but it's all about what we can afford at this point—

BETH: I just—

DAVID: What? [*Referring to the Realtor*] Just say it, she's downstairs staring into that pager of hers. Say it. I know what you're gonna say.

BETH [*whispering*]: I can't have Carl and Kevin thinking they don't have their own room at Mommy's house.

DAVID: And what about my kids?

BETH: I feel the same for them.

DAVID: Oh, you do?

BETH: Yes.

DAVID: The exact same.

BETH: David, don't start that again—

DAVID: Look, we both know, this is how much house we can afford right now, did we have the conversation or not? Did we sit there and add it all up or not?

BETH: David, if Carl and Kevin don't feel at home here now, if we don't make it a welcoming place for them now, they'll never feel like they belong.

DAVID: So what do you want me to do?

BETH: I don't know!

DAVID: If you know this is how much house we can afford, then what are you asking me to do?

BETH: I'm not . . . asking you to do anything!

DAVID: It seems like you are!

BETH: No, I just said I wish there were more bedrooms!

DAVID: Which is an indictment of me.

BETH: No, it's a fact.

DAVID: No, it's not, it's an indictment of me.

BETH: Would you stop? We're choosing to do this and it's . . . it's just hard to face the limits of it, that's all.

DAVID: And the limits are set by the fact I don't make enough money to buy a house with six bedrooms, or however many you think would be enough for everyone to feel "at home"! It's an indictment of me!

BETH: If you want to see it that way, for some sick, self-destructive reason—

DAVID: There's no other way to see it!

BETH: That's not true!

DAVID: Yes, it is! You don't want to work, so my salary is it, my salary is the border of what's possible—

BETH: I have told you I'm willing to work if it's—

DAVID: No! I don't want you coming home every day, tired and miserable, and blaming it on me! He didn't make you work, I'm not gonna make you work. I won't have you hating me for that. Shit.

[*He sits on the bed.*]

Isn't this fun.

[*Brief pause.*]

My kids would like their own rooms too, you know.

BETH: I know.

[*Brief pause.*]

DAVID: Shit shit shit.

BETH: I'm sorry I brought it up.

DAVID: To have to . . . to have to be in this situation at this point in my life . . . to be starting everything over is just really discouraging sometimes, you know?

BETH: I think it's sort of fun.

DAVID: Then why do you bring up impossible things I can't do anything about? If it's so fun?

BETH: I wasn't—

DAVID: You don't think it's fun, anyway, that's a shitty patronizing thing to say.

BETH: If I can't be honest with you about what I care about, David, then who can I talk to about it? Who?

DAVID: You can talk to me, but could you do it without accusing me of keeping your kids from feeling at home?

BETH: I never said—

[*Brief pause.*]

Forget it.

[*Longer pause.*]

Look. Do you like this house?

DAVID: I like it OK. I wish we could get something bigger too, something closer to the lake, like your place—

BETH: But given all that, do you like this house?

DAVID: Yeah, I like it. I like the trees.

BETH: Then let's buy it.

DAVID: No, it doesn't have enough bedrooms.

BETH: David—

DAVID: No, look, you're right, it doesn't have enough bedrooms—

BETH: David, stop. Listen. We'll have a summit meeting with the kids. And we'll let them decide together how to decorate that other bedroom, we'll get two bunk beds, we'll let them divide up the drawers, we'll put them in charge of everything. What we can't give them in terms of space, we'll give them in terms of autonomy.

DAVID: Don't try to make it better.

BETH: I'm not.

DAVID: Yes, you are, you're being like a prairie wife.

BETH: And you're being kind of a jerk.

DAVID: Look, I'm sorry, but I didn't fall in love with you so you could be brave and resourceful. I wanted to give you things and treat you better than your asshole husband, not . . . force you to make excuses for why we can't treat your kids like members of the family.

BETH: Your kids, too.

DAVID: I know, but I can carry that, I've been disappointing my kids ever since they were born. Disappointing you is a new feeling. And I don't like it.

BETH: You want to go back to our kingdom in the clouds.

DAVID: I wouldn't mind.

BETH: With the apples like tall ships, sailing . . .

DAVID: It was better. It was simpler.

BETH: No it wasn't. We were lying all the time and sneaking around.

DAVID: I didn't mind the lying.

BETH: I did.

DAVID: You would've gotten used to it.

BETH: No, I was nervous all the time, and rushing around trying to fit you into my schedule . . . I never got the grocery shopping really totally done the whole time we were seeing each other . . . it was hell.

DAVID: But now you get it done.

BETH: Yes!

DAVID: That's great. Christ, I can feel it starting all over again.

BETH: What does that mean?

DAVID: Just what you said, Beth, it's exactly what you said. We've done it, we've become like them. We're the ones who break up families and buy shitty furniture to fill up ugly houses, we're the ones who ruin the world all for the chance to have sex with someone we want to have sex with.

[*Brief pause.*]

Don't look that way.

BETH: Is that what you think this is?

DAVID: Isn't it? I mean, I have feelings, but underneath the feelings, what else is it?

BETH: It's love, I thought—

DAVID: "Love."

BETH: I thought that's what it was anyway.

DAVID [*overlapping*]: Love that tears everything in its path apart. Love that deprives innocent children of their parents.

BETH: Oh my God . . .

DAVID: Don't get that tone in your voice, please. It's so fucking dramatic.

BETH: I knew this would happen . . .

DAVID: Beth, would you please spare me your fragility just this once, just this once?

BETH: I have left my children—

DAVID: I've left mine too!

BETH: Don't tell me I can't have feelings about that, about how much I've set aside!

DAVID: See, this is how it starts, we're not even in the goddamn house and it's "how much you've set aside" . . .

BETH: David, if you're not comfortable with thinking you're worth it—

DAVID: Don't make it about me!

BETH: Then what—

DAVID: It's what we have together, if it's anything, but I can't take it being about me!

BETH: Then what we have together—

DAVID: Which it might not even *be*—

BETH: If you can't live with what it costs me to be with you, then we shouldn't do this!

DAVID [*loud*]: Maybe you're right, maybe we shouldn't!

[*Long silence.*]

[*Quieter*] Maybe it's all a big mistake.

[*Brief pause.*]

When I sat Gus down and told him I was moving out . . . you know what I felt? I felt . . . this is terrible to even say . . . I felt . . . I enjoyed making him sad.

BETH: No, you didn't—

DAVID: Yes, I did, that's who I am now, I was being all sympathetic but inside I was saying, "See, you little shit, this is how hard it's been for me ever since the day you were born and cemented me into this marriage; now you live with it for a while and see how it feels." I felt that feeling behind the words; behind all the sadness and sympathy, there was just . . . smallness.

BETH: I don't believe that.

DAVID: You don't feel any resentment at all . . . towards them?

BETH: Of course I do, David, they're my kids! But it's been . . . I know you don't want to hear things like this, because I'm not supposed to feel anything that makes you feel guilty, but . . . living without those guys is breaking my heart, resentment and all, it's breaking my heart! I thought I knew what heartbroken was—

DAVID: But being with me has taught you.

BETH: That's not what I'm saying—

DAVID: But that's what the situation *is*!

BETH: You know, *you're* the one a person can't say anything around, you're the one who's fragile—

DAVID: I'm the one who's realistic!

BETH: *Then it's too late to be realistic!*

DAVID: No, it's not! You can go back to Brad.

BETH: I don't want to go back to Brad!

DAVID: You want to go back to your boys!

BETH: Yes, I do! But I can't!

DAVID: Why? Just go back! Suck it up! Deal with it! I certainly don't want to spend the rest of my life with someone who's this unhappy!

BETH: Neither do I!

DAVID: Then go back! Why don't you just go back?

BETH [*whispering fiercely, full of hate and desperation*]: *Because I'm pregnant, you fucking jerk, you selfish selfish selfish fucking jerk! Because I'm pregnant.*

[*Brief pause. He reaches out to her.*]

Don't. Don't touch me. Don't you ever . . . ever . . . ever touch me again.

[*She wipes her eyes as she cries.*]

God. I'm so alone.

[*Brief pause.* DAVID *goes to her. He moves to put his arms around her.*]

No.

DAVID: Come on. I'm sorry. Come on. Please. Please. I'm sorry.

[*She moves closer to him. He very gently puts his arms around her.*]

BETH: It's all so hard.

DAVID: Yeah. It is.

[*They hold each other for a long moment. Then they both look up suddenly toward where the door to the room would be.*]

BETH: Shit.

[*They step apart.* BETH *wipes her eyes, pulling herself together.*]

Here she comes.

SCENE 9

[BETH *exits the bedroom area.* DAVID *picks up the stuffed tiger from the bedside table and then steps into a pool of light downstage.*]

DAVID: Dear Lily.

[*Music rises.*]

Life goes by so quickly I thought I would take a moment today to sit down and write you a letter. You can't read yet, but I am going to put this in the box Mommy keeps all your pictures in, and you can read it when you're older. Long before you were born, Mommy used to have dreams about you. And she would tell them to me, and we would have so much fun sitting quietly, talking about what you'd be like. It was almost as if you were our friend before you were ever really here. Of course, we didn't really know you then. We didn't know your first word would be "purple" or that you would like eating lamb so much or that you would be such a great singer. It has been a real treat to find out all the ways we were wrong about you and right about you, and you continue to surprise us every day. Lately, when we put you to bed, you make us say, "Tweety tweety, co-co-coconut, ga ga goo goo, bo bo bo bo, I love you, see you in the morning, sleep well, good night, sleep tight, don't let the bedbugs bite, that's right, that's all, sweet dreams, work well, think twice." And we don't know where you came up with this from.

Today is a very special day, because it is Christmas Eve. You are so excited! You have asked Santa for a Barbie doll, a puppy, and a tiger—we'll see what happens. But the best news is, today one of Mommy's dreams about you came true. We went to the store this afternoon, and the traffic was very busy and it was snowing, and we got flour and butter and sugar to make cookies. And we got something very strange called orange flower water, to make the cookies smell pretty. In Mommy's dream, you spilled the orange flower water in the backseat—we didn't know then that you would be a good girl who wouldn't do that—but we rolled down the windows anyway as we drove back to our apartment and poured out some of it on the seats, and we were all so happy our hearts almost flew out of us and took off.

[*Light shift and* CATHY, BRAD, *and* BETH *rise and step downstage, aware of* DAVID, *but facing the audience, their varying degrees of implacability standing in contrast to whatever small note of unadulterated positivity* DAVID *strikes.*]

What also was different today from Mommy's dream is it was a little sad. Because Mommy and Daddy hurt a lot of people's feelings, and made your half brothers and half sisters very sad, just for the chance to be together. And they all visited us this morning, and you cried when they left, because you love them so much and they are very sweet to you. And this is one of life's great mysteries, Lily, my dear little pumpkin seed, and I cannot explain it, but somehow people are always hurting each other and love keeps happening. It just keeps happening. And the longer you live and the more you notice this, the harder it gets to know what's right and wrong. Sometimes it almost seems impossible. All I know is we would not change anything that ever happened, ever, because I am so excited to know you and Mommy and we can't wait to see what you are going to do with your amazing life.

[BRAD, CATHY, *and* BETH *leave the stage as* DAVID *continues.*]

So. That's all. I am wrapping this letter around this little bottle of orange flower water—(Mommy's cookies didn't really turn out so good)—so you can smell it again when you are bigger and you want to remember all the mixed-up reasons that go into making a miracle like you. Whatever happens to you ever in this life, always remember we love you, Lily, and you are worth *everything*.

[*A moment passes.* DAVID *puts the stuffed tiger on the bed and exits. Lights slowly fade. A pool of light lingers on the tiger as the music rises. Blackout.*]

THE PAVILION

"I guessed the wrong keys, I battered on the wrong panels, I picked the wrong roads. O God, ain't there no way to guess again and start all over back where I had the keys in my hands, back where the roads all came together and I had my pick?"
   —from "Ambassadors of Grief" by Carl Sandburg

Pavilion *n*. 1. An ornate tent. 2. A light, sometimes ornamental roofed structure used at parks or fairs for amusement or shelter. 3. A temporary structure erected at a fair or a show. 4. The surface of a brilliant-cut gem.

PRODUCTION HISTORY

The Pavilion was originally produced by City Theatre Company in Pittsburgh, Pennsylvania, in 2000 and partially developed at the Carnegie Mellon School of Drama. It was directed by Aaron Posner; the set design was by Tony Ferrieri; the lighting design was by William O'Donnell; the costume design was by Lorraine Venberg; the sound design was by Jennifer Fritsch; the original guitar music was by Craig Wright; and the production stage manager was Patti Kelly. The guitar music was performed by Tom Cunningham. The cast was as follows:

Narrator .... Joel Van Liew
Peter .... J. Christopher O'Connor
Kari .... Kathryn Petersen

The Pavilion had its New York premiere at the Rattlestick Playwrights Theater (David Van Asselt, artistic director; Sandra Coudert, managing director). It was directed by Lucie Tiberghien; the set design was by Takeshi Kata; the lighting design was by Matt Richards; the costume design was by Mimi O'Donnell; the composer and pianist was Christophe Tiberghien; the production stage manager was Paige Van Den Burg; and the assistant stage manager was Libby Steiner. The cast was as follows:

Narrator .... Stephen Bogardus
Peter .... Brian D'Arcy James
Kari .... Jennifer Mudge

CHARACTERS

Narrator, *who also plays various characters*
Peter, *a thirty-seven-year-old man*
Kari, *a thirty-seven-year-old woman*

SCENE

The play takes place at the Pavilion, an old dance hall in the fictional town of Pine City, Minnesota. The setting is suggested only by a pair of benches. The time is the present.

SONG CREDIT

"Down in the Ruined World," music by Peter Lawton and Craig Wright, lyrics by Craig Wright. For sheet music, see appendix, page 149.

ACT 1

NARRATOR [*to the audience*]: This is the way the universe begins. A raindrop (that isn't really a raindrop) drops, like a word, "rain" *drops,* into a pool (that isn't really a pool, more like a pool of listening minds), and tiny waves circle out in an elegant decelerating procession, -cession, -cession. Then, after a time, the pool of listening minds grows still once more.

Now, but *backwards,* this is the way the universe begins: the still pool of listening minds, the sudden shrinking circles dissolving at the center, conserving at the center until boom, sloop!, up sends the droplet, up towards the voice that raindrops words, up towards the voice and it hangs in the air—remember it there—because *that's* the way the universe begins. A little pavilion. A momentary sphere. A word made of stars, dancing.

From the fire-latticed floor of the earth, sweet shoots of green spring up through the cooling webs, and mountain deep water sloshes over continents, swinging. Volcanoes of ice snow crystal-blue ash across miles of moss-seething tundra, and creatures crawl up on the shore, imagining things. The air is blood-thick with insect songs and the palm fronds tinkle like gongs in the tropical rain. Monkeys in slow motion turn into women and men and soon campfires dot the plains for days in every direction. And around each campfire, minds spring to life like sudden stars in a blank, black sky. The tiny tea leaf of consciousness spreads its bittersweet smoke through the sea of the primitive mind. Law is invented; then morality, then love, then forgiveness. Thousands and thousands of ideas, knit together over time, each one less practical and more ornamental than the last, all stretched taut above the wandering, wondering heads like a little pavilion; a temporary shelter for the human project.

[PETER *enters, holding a spray of flowers.*]

Once secured, time speeds up like a language being learned. Very quickly, like words and ideas forming in a mind, African empires rise and fall, greatness sprays up in fountains all across the Fertile Crescent and then shatters into droplets of novelty and nuance; Alexander and his Macedonians hammer through Persia, Asia Minor, deep into India, and blood and knowledge spread machine-like through the valleys, float down the Ganges on a bed of simmering pollen, algae, and dharma. Christ is born, and a second later, nailed to a tree; Europe is invented and then the Renaissance and then the Enlightenment and then the steam engine and then suddenly!—*his family* came to Minnesota in the late 1800s. From Finland. His great-great-grandmother wrote a book which is actually in the Library of Congress, about her first winter in the New World. Anyone can read it, it's there. It's called *Pioneer Days*. Years came and went, faster and faster, there were two world wars, one right after another, and then he was born right here in Pine City, Minnesota, in the year we call 1967 in the house across the bay there, on the shore of Lake Melissa, that's *you*, and this . . . this is the Pavilion.

[*The* NARRATOR *indicates the stage.*]

The windowed walls of this century-old dance hall are all opened out toward the lake. The tables are set, the floor's been swept, and the napkins are folded like fans in the water glasses. There's a cool breeze blowing, and every now and then the buzz and hum of water-skiers passing by can be heard through the dinner music being piped in over the sound system. [*To the* TECHS] Excuse me, could we have some dinner music, please? And a water-skier, perhaps? Thank you.

[*To the audience*] This is a play. About time. It's seven o'clock. Ten or twenty couples have already arrived. Some are milling about, some are seated at their tables, reading their place mats, upon which are printed "The Class of 1985's Hall of Fame." That was twenty years ago. The Boy Most Likely to Succeed is now a Microsoft millionaire. The Girl with the Best Sense of Humor is still single. And one half of the Cutest Senior Couple is suddenly picked out of the crowd by a friend. [*To* PETER] Peter Mollberg?

PETER: Pudge?! Is that you?

NARRATOR [*as* PUDGE]: It's me!

PETER: You've lost weight!

NARRATOR: You know what, I haven't! My body has changed, but I still weigh the same!

PETER: You look great, though!

NARRATOR: That's what everybody keeps telling me! I'll take it! Hey, I read in the program book, Peter, you and me, we're in the same business!

PETER: You're a psychologist?

NARRATOR: Yeah, I kinda am!

PETER: What does that mean?

NARRATOR: I'm working nights at the Suicide Hotline!

PETER [*befuddled*]: That's great!

NARRATOR: Yeah, I got started volunteering through church, but it turns out I'm really good at it! So I quit the turkey farm and they hired me on full-time with benefits! A nationwide company!

PETER: Congratulations.

NARRATOR: Yeah, the guy in charge took me in the office and said, "You know, I've never seen anything like it, Pudge, you've got a natural ability for this sort of stuff."

PETER: I bet you do.

NARRATOR: He said I've got a comforting presence, and that's what it takes, right? [*Suddenly, grimly, as* KENT] Hey, has either of you guys seen Cookie?

PETER: No.

NARRATOR [*as* KENT]: Thanks.

PETER: Pudge, I'm a little confused . . .

NARRATOR: What?

PETER: How do they make money on an 800 number?

NARRATOR: Aha! It's not an 800 number, Peter. It's a 900 number.

PETER: Ahh.

NARRATOR: Yeah, ninety-nine cents a minute.

PETER: For a suicide hotline?

NARRATOR: Man, when it works, it's a bargain!

PETER: You don't get a *lot* of calls, do you?

NARRATOR: Only thousands. And not all from around here either. Like last night, I was just slammed. Didn't even get a break! This one guy, his name was Kevin Conzemius from Fresno, California . . . what a sad sack, he kept me on the phone for two hours, this guy, with a gun to his head the whole time!

PETER [*adding it up, horrified*]: That's 120 bucks . . .

NARRATOR: Yeah, ka-ching! See, he went out to California from Louisville, where he was from, with this girl, Kendra, and then she left him for some guy and he was really freaked out. I mean, I think he had some pretty deep-seated self-esteem problems going way back.

PETER: Sounds like it, going to California.

NARRATOR: That's what I told him too! What a freak! But every minute or so, Peter, he was interrupting me, tapping the barrel on the telephone, saying, "You're not listening to me, man! *You're not listening to me!!!*" And then BANG!

PETER: What happened?

NARRATOR: That's confidential, Peter; you understand.

[KARI *enters, catching* PETER's *eye.*]

You know, after the reunion, they're gonna burn the old place down, right?

PETER [*distracted by* KARI]: The Pavilion?

NARRATOR: Yeah, the fire department's gonna burn it down.

PETER: Why?

NARRATOR: Because starting tomorrow, they're gonna build a big concrete amphitheater.

PETER: For Summer Carnival?

NARRATOR: No, there's gonna be a five-day country music festival here every summer from now until 2028.

PETER: Jesus.

NARRATOR: Yeah, Cookie Brustad's mayor now, Peter, everything's changing. Everything's changing. Who are the flowers for?

PETER: Kari.

NARRATOR [*as in "bad idea"*]: Ohhh . . .

KARI: Denise!

[*The* NARRATOR *becomes* DENISE.]

NARRATOR [*as* DENISE]: Kari!

KARI: You are the last person I expected to see here tonight! The world traveler! You didn't even come to the ten-year!

NARRATOR: I tried!

KARI: You did not!

NARRATOR: No, I had the date mixed up, I came a week early.

KARI: That is a lie!

NARRATOR: No, I swear, I showed up at the Dude Ranch, and there were all these people wearing chaps and spurs and I was thinking, "Boy, everyone's really changed . . ."

KARI: Oh my God, that is so funny.

NARRATOR: Give me a hug.

[*They hug and make an "MMMMMM" hug sound.*]

KARI: I'm so glad you came.

NARRATOR: Where's Hans?

KARI: Home sick.

NARRATOR: Aww.

KARI: But I want to know what *you've* been up to; last I heard you were in . . . Thailand or somewhere?

NARRATOR: Bangkok, mm-hmm.

KARI: God, that's so cool. Doing what?

NARRATOR: Drug enforcement. Working for the embassy.

KARI: That must be so exciting.

NARRATOR: It's not so different from Pine City. *Lot* of drugs. And you're . . .

KARI: . . . still at the bank.

NARRATOR [*weakly*]: Wow.

KARI: I've tried to get out, Denise, but they keep me locked up with all the valuables down there in the basement—

NARRATOR: You're still in the safety deposit box?

KARI: Yeah, but hey, I spend my days surrounded by diamonds and pearls, it could be worse . . .

NARRATOR: And you're still with Hans.

KARI: I am, yeah.

NARRATOR: And how's that?

KARI: Fine.

NARRATOR: Really?

KARI [*reassuring* DENISE]: Hans is not so bad, Denise. In fact, do you want to know what the only bad part is, of being married to Hans, the only bad part?

NARRATOR: What?

KARI: And you can't tell anybody ever that I said this, OK?

NARRATOR: What is it?

KARI [*almost whispering*]: I really hate golf. Isn't that awful? I didn't know it when I married him, I was actually thinking it might be kinda fun to live on a golf course and be married to the pro, you know? I don't know, you know, all the grass, maybe, it just seemed . . . pastoral. But now I know, I hate golf.

NARRATOR: I do too . . .

KARI: And you should see it, Denise, our house is so full of tees—

NARRATOR: I can imagine—

KARI: —and balls and visors and clubs, it's so—

NARRATOR: Golfy—

KARI: Yes, and he has this putting green set up in the rec room that he practices on every night and I swear, the sound of that ball popping out of that machine, it's like a baby spitting up.

NARRATOR: Do you two have any kids?

KARI: No, we've got a dog, though, Tramp, he's our big baby.

NARRATOR [*conspiratorially*]: Peter's here.

KARI: Who cares?

[*Beat.*]

So, uh . . . are *you* married or . . . whatever . . . involved with . . . anybody?

[PETER *and* KARI *see each other for the first time.*]

NARRATOR [*as* NARRATOR, *to the audience*]: At the center of everything in the universe, there's you.

PETER: Hi.

KARI: Hi.

NARRATOR [*to the audience*]: A fragile crystal (that isn't a crystal, really, more like a way of being), spinning and changing, gathering and giving off light. And this method, this bright idea that is YOU is displayed, like a jewel, in a body. Your body.

PETER [*tentatively*]: How are you doing?

KARI: I'm fine.

NARRATOR [*to the audience*]: And beyond the edge of your body lie the gem-like worlds, each one nested snugly in the next; the world of air, the world of people, the world of emotions, of ideas, of the sky, of fire, of the stars, of cold darkness and mystery; and nothingness. And at the center of everything in the universe, there's you—this force, sending out trajectories, creating webs of relationship with your words, with your work, with your love. It seems so simple, and yet, there are these *other people*—

PETER: You haven't changed a bit.

KARI [*uncomfortably*]: Yes, I have.

NARRATOR [*to the audience*]: —every one of them *also* a center of everything, every one of them *also* cradled and maintained at the hub of all existence—

PETER: I just mean you look great.

KARI [*coldly matter-of-fact*]: Thanks.

NARRATOR [*to the audience*]: —just like you and yet, not you.

KARI: You look tired.

PETER: I've been driving all day.

NARRATOR [*to the audience*]: An infinite number of centers to an infinite number of worlds; but you can stand right next to them and talk. It all makes for quite a complex geometry. And then there's time. It's seven thirty-five.

[PETER *offers the bouquet.*]

PETER: I got you these.

KARI [*not taking them*]: Why?

PETER: I don't know . . . I ran into Slick at Sundberg's Café, he walked me down the street, showed me around the flower shop, I thought of you. That's all. Don't feel like you have to take them.

KARI: I don't.

PETER: See, that's cool. [*Making conversation*] I guess marrying into that family was the smartest thing Slick ever did, huh . . .

KARI: Yeah, Slick's a real genius.

PETER: All I mean is he owns that place now, and he never would've—

KARI: Half.

PETER: What?

KARI: He only owns half.

PETER: He told me he owns it all.

KARI: Once Jackie's mom dies, but not until then.

PETER: He told me point-blank she's dead and he owns it.

KARI: That's what he tells everybody.

PETER: While Jackie's mother's still alive?

KARI: Yeah, you didn't tell him those were for me, did you?

PETER: No.

KARI: Because that wouldn't be good.

[*Brief pause.*]

PETER: How's Hans?

KARI [*closing up*]: Hans is fine. How's your dad?

PETER: I'm just trying to be polite.

KARI: Nice try.

PETER: Didn't mean to make you mad.

KARI [*mad*]: I'm not mad! I just really wish you'd let me know you were coming.

PETER: Why?

KARI: Because I wouldn't have come, OK, I wouldn't have come. Are you gonna stay?

PETER: Why?

KARI: Because if you're gonna stay, then I won't.

PETER: Then I won't stay.

[*Beat.*]

KARI: No, don't do me any favors, if you want to stay, you stay, just don't ... talk to me or anything or talk to my friends, OK?

PETER: OK.

[*Beat.*]

KARI: Actually, do whatever you want, because I don't want to be involved with you, I don't want to be here with you NOT doing something because of me, so just be here and whatever ... happens ... happens! OK?

PETER: OK.

KARI: Good!

PETER: That went well.

NARRATOR [*as* NARRATOR]: It's eight o'clock. Dinner's in full swing. Toasts are being made so vigorously by this time that already by the entrance to the catering truck there's a bus pan full of broken glass. The sun is setting across the lake in a golden purple mist—if you're seated by the stage, you can see it from there—and everyone in the room is bathed in warm summer air and *the most poetic lavender light.* [*To the* TECHS, *after the stage turns a bit lavender*] Thank you. [*To the audience*] It's really very grand.

KARI: And then he has the nerve to show up with flowers, it just blows my mind!

[*The* NARRATOR *becomes* ANGIE.]

NARRATOR [*as* ANGIE, *troubled*]: Maybe he's changed.

KARI: People don't change.

NARRATOR: Maybe he wants to change.

KARI: No, I know what he wants, Angie, he wants to be a good guy. He wants everybody to say, "Wouldja look at that ... Peter and Kari! Boy he must really feel bad about dumping her when she was pregnant, but gee, it looks like she's found it in her heart after all these years blah blah blah blah blah," I don't want to do that!!

NARRATOR: Do you have a Kleenex?

KARI [*absently*]: Yeah, here—I don't want to spend this whole evening having people whisper in my ear, "Peter's here, did you see, Peter's here, are you gonna talk to Peter?"

NARRATOR: But he looks so lost.

KARI: That's because he is, he shouldn't be here! I mean, if you're gonna live by a certain set of rules, then live by them; but don't come crawling back, don't try to change the rules later just because you feel bad—

NARRATOR: Why?

KARI: —what?

NARRATOR: Why not change the rules? Why not try, if you're not happy?

KARI: Because, you should live with what you did. You did it, you suffer, you live with it.

NARRATOR: But that's why I'm . . .

KARI: What?

NARRATOR: That's why I'm seeing Cookie now. I'm changing the rules because I'm not happy. Kent doesn't make me happy.

KARI: But it's different—

NARRATOR: You told me you thought it was a good idea . . .

KARI: For you, Angie. For you.

NARRATOR: But not for Peter.

KARI: Not for me.

[ANGIE *bursts into tears.*]

What, Angie? What is it?

NARRATOR: I'm pregnant.

KARI: Is it Cookie's?

NARRATOR: I don't know.

KARI: Oh my God.

[*The* NARRATOR *becomes* NOLAN.]

NARRATOR [*as* NOLAN]: I was sitting around a campfire with about five or six of my Roman centurions. Peter, it was so real.

PETER: Sounds like it.

NARRATOR: We were camped in a wide valley in the Caucasus Mountains. For hundreds of yards in every direction I could see fires and circles of my soldiers and I could hear horses whinnying out in the darkness.

[*He does two distant whinnies and a snort.*]

And there was a goat, roasting over the fire on a spit. I could hear the fat crackling and smell the meat. It was amazing. And I looked around at my men and I suddenly knew they were all going to die in the midst of battle the very next day. And I was the only one who knew.

PETER: That does sound pretty amazing.

NARRATOR: So yeah, I believe in it. Kari really hates your guts.

PETER: Yeah.

NARRATOR: She doesn't believe in reincarnation either. You two *should* be together.

PETER: She's married to Hans.

NARRATOR: In *this* life.

KARI: Peter's gotten kinda fat, hasn't he?

[*The* NARRATOR *becomes* CORAL.]

NARRATOR [*as* CORAL]: Fat? No. Are you gonna eat that?

KARI: But look at him; he's gotten kind of . . . pushy-mushy, hasn't he?

NARRATOR [*chewing*]: Don't be mean, he's just older, Kari. We're all older. And what is he, a counselor or something like that? He never moves, he sits in a chair all day.

[*She takes another morsel.*]

These are so good! [*Chewing*] I think you're being too hard on him. You're no spring chicken either.

KARI: I sit in a chair all day down in the box at the bank and I weigh the same as I did in high school.

NARRATOR: Only because you're sad. That's not a good thing. Look at all the gals. Heather, Alison. If you'd had some kids like we did—oh shit I'm sorry—[*As* KENT] Hey, have you seen Cookie? Or Angie?

KARI: They were, he was right over there by the punch bowl, Kent, uh, a moment ago. And I haven't seen Angie recently.

NARRATOR [*as* KENT]: Thanks. [*As* CORAL] I'm sorry, I don't know why I said that. [*As* NARRATOR] It's eight thirty-two. The dinner dishes have been cleared away by the teenagers in their black pants and white shirts, thirty-five dollars for one night of work. And there's a woman standing on the stage, talking into a microphone that obviously isn't working, and then suddenly, with a pop and a squeal, it is.

[*The* NARRATOR *becomes* LISA. *Note: the year of the graduating class that* LISA *mentions can be moved forward to reflect the change in production date.*]

NARRATOR [*as* LISA, *to the audience*]: Is everybody having a good time? Fabulous! For those of you who don't know me, I'm Lisa Gulbranson, and I know you've all been here for a while, having a wonderful dinner and catching up with each other, but now let me formally welcome you, on behalf of the whole reunion committee (which is essentially me and Angie) to the Class of 1985's Twentieth Reunion! Yay! There's some school spirit! Pine City Panthers, P-C-P! I see a lot of familiar faces out there! And don't everybody forget we've got Skippy Schouviller from Ingebretsen Photography set up right over there all night taking pictures, so if you want your picture taken with the *old gang*, you just talk to him.

Now, when we first started planning this party, Angie and I thought it would be fabulous if we could get "The Mustangs" back together to play. But it didn't take long for us to realize only two of the original Mustangs were still with us: Eddie Gieselhardt and Peter Mollberg. Then we never got an RSVP from Peter . . . naughty. But, even *worse*, last month, as many of you probably have heard, Eddie was killed in a car accident on his way to a "gig" in Fargo. So when Peter called and told us last week he'd be coming, I asked him if he could just play us all a song, to remember and whatever, in Eddie's honor. So before we head into the dancing portion of the evening, let me introduce to you, and it makes me kinda sad to say this, the Class of 1985's vice president, and the only surviving member of The Mustangs, Peter Mollberg!

[PETER *enters with guitar.*]

PETER [*to the audience*]: Hey. It's nice to see everybody tonight. Uh, you'll have to imagine the rest of The Mustangs are up here with me. Spencer would've been over here on bass, Brad on the drums, and Eddie would've been right there. This, uh . . . this was the last song Eddie and I ever wrote. Ever since high school, we've been sending tapes back and forth in the mail, writing songs, just for fun. I wrote the words to this one and Eddie wrote the tune, and he would've played it a lot better than I'm gonna play it, but that's the breaks. Also, I gotta apologize a little bit, it's kind of a sad song, but this is a reunion, so that's OK, a little, right? So I figure this is Eddie's way of being here, and we can all get drunk and dance afterwards and he can't, so here it is. Nobody's ever heard this before. First time ever.

[*Singing*]

COME MY DARLING, COME MY LOVE
WE'LL GO DOWN IN THE RUINED WORLD
OF STRIP MALLS, CIGARETTES, RUBBER GLOVES
AND CALIFORNIA GIRLS.

IN EV'RY CORNER IN EV'RY CAR
THERE'S A COAL GREY COUPLE CURLED;
THE PEOPLE MAKE LOVE THE WAY THEY CAN
DOWN IN THE RUINED WORLD.

SO, COME MY ANGEL COME MY PRIZE
WE'LL GO DOWN IN THE RUINED WORLD.
DON'T VEIL YOUR FACE, DON'T HIDE YOUR EYES
SEE THE OIL IN THE WATER SWIRL.

THE SCENT'S ENOUGH TO SPIN YOUR HEAD,
BUT OH HOW THE COLORS CURL.
WE SETTLE FOR A BEAUTY SUNK IN CHAINS
DOWN IN THE RUINED WORLD.

AND WITH A LONELY KIND OF HEARTBREAK
WE LOOK AROUND, DO A DOUBLE TAKE.
IS IT BABYLON OR EDEN IN A MIST?
THERE'S NO WAY OF KNOWING.
IS THE GREAT WORLD JUST A BLACK HOLE
OR ETERNITY'S GREAT GOAL?

I FELT SURE OUR NAMES WERE ON THE LIST.
BUT WHERE ARE WE GOING?
DOWN IN THE RUINED WORLD.
THERE'S NO WAY OF KNOWING.
DOWN IN THE RUINED WORLD.
DOWN IN THE RUINED WORLD.

SO, COME MY DARLING, COME MY DEAR—
WE'LL GO DOWN IN THE RUINED WORLD.
WHERE THE ANSWERS ARE FOREVER NEAR
AND THEY'RE REAL AS CULTURED PEARLS.

IF THE WORLD IS WHAT THE EYE CAN SEE
THEN GOD'S A PRETTY GIRL,
AND THE ONLY FREEDOM IS TO GIVE
DOWN IN THE RUINED WORLD.
DOWN IN THE RUINED WORLD.
DOWN IN THE RUINED WORLD.
[*Spoken*] That's it. Thanks for listening. Mustangs forever!

NARRATOR [*as* NARRATOR]: It's nine o'clock, and the DJ is offering cash
prizes to the first ten couples to hit the dance floor. In far corners, squads
of men talk sports, play pinball, or network, and at least seven spouses,
who came only out of spite, have been abandoned and stand nursing their

drinks alone or in pairs along the cold, undecorated wall of a doomed land-mark which to them means nothing at all.

[*Music plays loudly while* NARRATOR, *as* PATTY, *and* KARI *dance.*]

NARRATOR [*as* PATTY]: So how come you're not dancing with you know who?

KARI [*not hearing*]: What?

NARRATOR: How come you're not dancing with *Peter*? Didn't you see the way he was looking at you from the stage?

KARI: Yes, I did, and that's one of the 15,000 reasons I'm not dancing with him!

NARRATOR: Do you still have any of Peter's songs?

KARI: No. I had one cassette with all the songs he ever wrote for me on it. But I got mad one day and broke it open and unspooled the whole thing.

NARRATOR: Kari! You are so fucking stupid.

KARI: I know! But I still have all the unwound tape. It's in a box at my folks', under my old bed, with some other stuff . . . pictures and things. But they're all torn up.

NARRATOR: But you've kept them?

KARI: I guess I have, yeah.

NARRATOR: Why, you fucking kookiehead?

KARI [*not hearing*]: What?

NARRATOR [*louder, as music stops*]: Why do you keep all of Peter's old pictures and songs if they're all torn up and destroyed? Are you still in love with Peter?

[KARI *exits the scene, mortified, as the* NARRATOR *becomes* SMOKE.]

PETER: I just think . . . I'm being honest now—I just think, I've had all these relationships, right?

NARRATOR [*as* SMOKE, *without interest*]: Yeah. Can I have a sip of that?

PETER: Here, and not one of them has ever really worked out. I mean, seri-ously, stop and think about this. Not one single relationship of mine has ever truly been healthy and normal and . . . right, as in, not even close! I look back . . . wreckage. Which is funny, I know, because I'm a psychologist so I'm supposed to have my shit together, OK, ha-ha. But I always get to a certain point, Smoke, where I just stop feeling. I go from everything and then suddenly to nothing, numbness, absolute zero.

NARRATOR: See, that's where I'm at with Theresa and the kids, exactly.

PETER: Why does that happen?

NARRATOR: It's just life, Peter, you get emptied out.

PETER: If you let yourself, maybe.

NARRATOR: No, you don't have any control, you're powerless. It's a physical thing, it's a natural degenerative process, like losing your hair. You lose your feelings.

PETER: No.

NARRATOR: *Yes.* Men are born with a certain capacity for feeling—like women, they've only got so many eggs—men only have so many feelings. And life uses them up. Every love affair, every death, every friend, every joke that's funny that we laugh at uses up our feelings. And when life's done with us, when it can't suck any more feelings out of us, life tosses us aside.

PETER: You really think so?

NARRATOR: Peter, I'm a minister. I know these things.

PETER: It's like . . .

NARRATOR [*bored*]: What?

PETER: No, you don't want to hear about this.

NARRATOR [*relieved*]: OK.

PETER: It's like when I said no to Kari back then, when I left town?

NARRATOR [*slightly impatient*]: Yeah?

PETER: It's like I got on the wrong train, you know? And I've been on this train now for twenty years, and Jesus, I don't want to go where this train is going, I really don't.

NARRATOR: Where do you want to go?

PETER: I want to go . . . I want to go where I maybe could have gone with her, you know? . . . if I had been more . . . I don't know, strong or something. When I saw Kari for the first time, Smoke, I'll never forget it; it was like the first or second week of high school and I walked into the audiovisual lab and there she was. And I swear—I couldn't have put this into words back then, but it's all I think about lately—it was really like I recognized her or something. And I don't mean it like we'd met before or anything. We'd never met. It was just . . . it was as if in her face . . . in her beauty . . . I was finally seeing the beauty of everything, you know? . . . the unreachable beauty of the whole world that I'd always felt inside and tried to hold on to but never could, it was all in her. The whole universe had articulated itself in her. To me. That's just how I saw it. And I just knew that if I could be with her . . . by her side, you know? . . . then I could be alive and be part of things. I'd at least have a chance. Now I know it sounds crazy, Smoke, I know, given everything that's happened, and there's a lot of water gone under the bridge, and a lot of time has passed, and there's been a lot of stupid shit and I've done most of it, but when I see her now, I still feel the same way. I look at her and I still see it, I see her face and I think, "Oh, there you are . . . the world. Where have you been?" I love her, you know? I screwed up back then, there's no getting around it, but I love her. I think she's great. I love her.

NARRATOR: Have you told her that?

PETER: No.

NARRATOR: Don't.

[*The* NARRATOR *becomes* CARLA.]

NARRATOR [*as* CARLA]: Whatever you do, honey, don't forgive him.

KARI: I'm not gonna forgive him!

NARRATOR: No, but I can see it in your eyes, you're susceptible. It was that song, wasn't it? Kari, just because Satan gave him that guitar to torment you with doesn't mean you have to take the bait like a dummy!

KARI: Carla, I'm just saying that I'm tired of being angry!

NARRATOR: Tough it out!

KARI: No!

NARRATOR: Yes, you tough it out! You stay angry! Because listen to me, honey, when you forgive a man you lose yourself, and that's the God's honest truth. You want some words to live by? Here's two: NEVER FORGIVE.

KARI: Carla . . .

NARRATOR: No, I'm right! Tim screwed around on me once—look at him over there, makes me sick—he screwed around on me with a girl we had working for the summer, this little bitch from Holland named Anna. [*Dutch accent*] Anna, Anna, Anna, Anna, *Anna*. [*Shudders*] And he begged me to forgive him, on his godforsaken knees in the parking lot at two in the morning, he begged me, crying like a baby, like he was awake having open heart surgery, "Oh I need you, Carla, please, please forgive me . . ."

KARI: Poor thing.

NARRATOR: That's exactly what I thought, and I forgave him. [*Hitting herself in the face*] Dummy! Worst thing I ever could have done. [*To* TIM] *Worst thing I ever could have done.* [*To* KARI] No, don't look at me that way, it's true, because ever since that day, I've been one down; and in marriage, honey, if you're one down, you're down all the way, and I know you know what I'm talking about.

KARI: What is that supposed to mean?

NARRATOR: Oh please. Christ, look at him over there. Makes me want to vomit. Someday, though—I tell you this in confidence—someday he's gonna do it again—he says he won't, but he will, he's weak, he will—and when he does I'm gonna take everything he's got along with the kids, and the first thing I'll do with the money—this is my dream, I think about it every night—the first thing I'll do is get myself a vanity plate and put it on my truck, and you know what it's gonna say? "I HATE TIM." You get eight letters—

KARI: Carla—

NARRATOR [*counting the letters*]: "I HATE TIM."

KARI: Carla!

NARRATOR: What?

KARI: You only get seven letters.

NARRATOR: Oh. Then it'll just have to be "HATE TIM." I think people will still get the idea.

KARI: Oh, I think they will too.

NARRATOR: Maybe they'd even take it as a challenge, you know? To get more involved?

KARI: Maybe.

NARRATOR: Like Greenpeace.

KARI: Gotcha.

NARRATOR: That'd be good. See, these reunions are *very* sneaky and the men know it too; they request the old songs from the DJ and talk about the old times, "Oh baby I've changed"; there's women feeling generous all over this place tonight. But listen to me, forgiving a man will not make you any younger; and, don't you dare dance that sweetheart dance with him, it's like giving yourself cancer indulging in that nonsense! Tim's asked me twice already and I've said no, and I'm married to him! Peter Mollberg hurt you. He didn't have to. He chose to do it. And that's the end of it. Christ, wouldja look at Tim over there? "Haw haw haw . . ." I swear I'm getting a case of infectious diarrhea just looking at him.

[*The* NARRATOR *becomes* COOKIE.]

NARRATOR [*as* COOKIE]: Peter Mollberg?!

PETER: Cookie?

NARRATOR: I've gained a lot of weight, I know, it's all the pot, man, I live in a state of continual munchies, but listen, you're a therapist or something in the Twin Cities, right?

PETER: Cookie, before we talk about anything else, we're gonna talk about the Pavilion—

NARRATOR: Now is not the time!

PETER: I heard on *Talk of the Nation* there are laws about landmarks and historic buildings—

NARRATOR: I heard the same show, Peter, but this is not a church, it's just the motherfucking Pavilion and the laws don't apply!

PETER: It's a church to me! This is a cathedral of memories in my head, and I bet it is to a lot of other people too—

NARRATOR: You know what it is to other people? It's a problem, it's old and in the way—

PETER: Yeah, well, I'm gonna call for a referendum—

NARRATOR: *We had a referendum, man, the people have already spoken, now would you please fucking listen to me?!!*

PETER: What is it?

NARRATOR [*heightening intensity of stoned paranoia*]: You're a shrink, right? Like you talk people down from buildings and stuff? You've got methods of ameliorating really high-pressure situations?

PETER: Why?

NARRATOR: I'm in totally deep shit, man. I'm desperate and on the run.

PETER: From who?

NARRATOR: Kent!

PETER: Kent Luneburg?

NARRATOR: Yeah! He found out about me and Angie and he called me this morning and said he's gonna kill me.

PETER: You're seeing Angie on the side?

NARRATOR: Duh! And Kent said he's gonna kill me tonight! Said Jesus told him it was all right!

PETER: Cookie, settle down! Have you called the police?

NARRATOR: He's the *chief* of police, Peter, get with the fucking program!

PETER: So what do you want me to do?

NARRATOR: *Talk* to him! "*Understand*" him, or whatever the fuck it is you people do!

[KARI *enters scene.*]

KARI: Cookie?

NARRATOR [*trying to be cool*]: Hey, Kari.

KARI: Kent's looking for you.

NARRATOR [*freaking out*]: *I know!* Peter, man, you gotta help me, he's stalking me like a fucking jungle cat!

PETER [*to* KARI]: Where is he?

KARI: He's right over there.

NARRATOR: Shit! All I want to do is make life better for people and smoke some decent weed and now I got fucking Jesus after my ass!

KARI: Jesus?

PETER: Kent says Jesus told him to kill Cookie.

KARI [*to* NARRATOR]: And you believe him?

NARRATOR: Well, what if Jesus really told him that, Kari? That's not good! Hey, is it true you guys are getting back together?

KARI: Are you telling people that?

PETER: No!

KARI [*to* COOKIE]: Where did you hear that?

NARRATOR: I don't know, it's just been kinda going around that Peter's moving back and Hans is outta the picture.

KARI: Shit! [*To* PETER] Have you been saying that to people?

PETER: No!

NARRATOR: Even if you're not moving back, you two *should* dance the sweetheart dance at midnight.

KARI: No, we shouldn't.

NARRATOR: But it'd be perfect, you guys were the Cutest Senior Couple and all that shit. We'll turn down the lights, turn on the glitter ball, give everybody a little hope for the future, you know? I mean, you guys were so fucked up, what a testament.

KARI: To *what*?

NARRATOR: Where is he now?

PETER: He went into the bathroom.

NARRATOR: Thank you, God.

[*The* NARRATOR *addresses the audience.*]

NARRATOR [*as* NARRATOR, *to the audience*]: It's nine thirty; the sun has gone down, and there's a warm corona of indiscriminate voices and sounds and grey-purple light that spreads for thirty yards in a circle around the old dance hall at the edge of the lake. Cars are beginning to cruise the lakeshore road . . . can you hear those radios? And the catering trucks are pulling away, having cleaned up the last of the dinnertime dishes; and the fire trucks are pulling up, groaning into the parking lot, and the hoses are being unrolled, and the crew of new volunteers, with "helmets and everything," are nervously awaiting their instructions in the quiet, spinning light of the silent sirens. And the party's still going strong.

PETER: Lot of people came.

KARI: Yeah.

PETER: More than I woulda thought.

KARI: Yeah, Angie and Lisa really got their shit together.

PETER: It's really a great party.

KARI: Yeah, it's a great party.

[*Beat.*]

PETER: So look, do you wanna . . . get out of here?

KARI: With you? Are you kidding me?

PETER: I'm not, actually.

NARRATOR [*as* JEFF]: Hey, Peter, that song was beautiful, man!

PETER: Thanks! [*To* KARI] I thought maybe we could . . . you're looking at me funny, is this the craziest thing anybody's ever said to you?

KARI: It's close.

PETER: I almost forgot, I got you these.

[*He offers her a small box of chocolates.*]

KARI: God, Peter, you're like Monty Hall. What are they?

PETER: Just some chocolates. With caramel. Your favorite.

[*She does not take the box.*]

NARRATOR [*as* SARAH]: Kari, Darren and I are going home, do you want us to drop you off on the way?

KARI: No, I've got a car, Sarah, thanks!

NARRATOR: You're OK to drive?

KARI: Uh-huh.

NARRATOR [*doubtful*]: OK.

PETER: Come on, we'll just get the hell out of here and go have a drink at the Shoreview or something. Nothing romantic.

KARI: Like it's up to you whether it's romantic.

PETER: I'm just saying my intentions are honorable.

KARI: Are you nuts?

PETER: No, listen, it'll be nice. We'll play some air hockey and see Cork and Patty and the Ruika Brothers. We'll say hi to Frostie and Booger. We'll just check it out and then I'll take you home. No big deal. Please.

KARI: Peter. The Shoreview was torn down three years ago. There's a waterslide there now. Cork and Patty broke up. Cork is working on a fishing boat up in Alaska and Patty and the three kids, one with leukemia, are living with Patty's mom in Staples. The Ruika Brothers are in jail for robbing the bank in Wadena. Booger is dead—

NARRATOR [*as* ARNE]: Kari, would you tell Hans I'm gonna be late for my tee time tomorrow, I'm so fucked up.

KARI: Yeah, Arne, I'll tell him—

NARRATOR: Thanks. Hey, Peter, I love you!

PETER [*disconcerted*]: Hi.

KARI: —and I don't want you to take me home.

PETER [*astonished*]: Booger's dead?

KARI: Yeah, he fell from six stories working construction up in Grand Forks after the flood in ninety-nine.

PETER: Jesus.

NARRATOR [*as* CARL]: Yo, Peter, Mustangs forever!

PETER [*distractedly*]: Yeah, Carl, rock on! [*To* KARI] Sorry about that.

KARI: No, it was a nice song.

PETER: Kari, what do I have to do to get that look off your face so you can see me? This is not twenty years ago, I'm not who I was; can't we just be together for a couple of minutes to talk as human beings? I'm not asking you to hold my hand or anything—

[*She holds up her hand with the wedding ring on it.*]

KARI: Peter, look! Does this ring mean anything to you? Does it signify anything at all? I'm married, OK? I'm attached. Vowed. Wedded. Welded. I'm married!

PETER: It's OK with Hans.

KARI: What do you mean it's OK with Hans?

PETER: Just that, it's OK with Hans, if that's what you're worried about.

KARI: You called Hans, what, you e-mailed him?

PETER: I called him at the pro shop.

KARI: Are you fucking kidding me?

PETER: No.

KARI: Oh my God. So, OK, you called him and asked him what?

PETER: I just asked if I could maybe see you after the reunion, to try to clear some things up—he knows we knew each other—

KARI: I know he knows we knew each other, everyone in town knows we knew each other! God, are you really as stupid as this? Or as devious? Shit!

PETER: He wasn't in our class, he said he wasn't going. It's better that way, isn't it, that he knows? Otherwise I felt out of line, you know?

KARI: Do you know how creepy that is, to call my husband? How invasive?

PETER: I was trying to do the right thing for *you*—

KARI: So you called my husband and asked him, what? For permission to take me out or something?

PETER: Sort of, I guess, yeah . . .

KARI: Grow up!

PETER: Look, I thought it was a good idea, maybe I was wrong!

KARI: There's no maybe about it, Peter, you were wrong!

PETER: I'm sorry!

KARI: God, I've been sitting here all night going nuts thinking of what to do, trying to decide what position it would put me in with Hans if I even talked to you, if he knew, if he didn't, and what that would mean, and now you tell me that you called him and he knows—you asshole!

PETER: I said I'm sorry!

KARI: Saying you're sorry doesn't change the position I've been put in! "Sorry" isn't even a word! "Sorry" is just a noise people make when nothing else can happen! God, do you know what it's gonna be like when I go home tonight? What I'm going to have to wade through? Shit! You are always doing this to me! Do me a favor and just go away! I mean it, go away! *Move apart from me!*

NARRATOR [*as* JAKE]: Kari, are you OK?

KARI: I'm fine! I'm fine.

PETER: I just didn't want to get you in trouble with Hans!

KARI: I'm his wife, not his daughter!

PETER: You know what I mean.

KARI: Yes, I do know what you mean, you mean you didn't want to get yourself in trouble with Hans. Or maybe you did, I don't know, you're such a weirdo! Anyway, Peter, let's just get the cards on the table, even if I wasn't married, even if you were the last man on earth, I wouldn't go with you to the Shoreview or even for a walk around the block, OK?

PETER: Kari, I know I hurt you, that's why I'm here—

KARI: "Hurt"? "Hurt" barely touches this, Peter, this is not about being "hurt." There's a pain beyond hurt; and it's vast and it's endless and it doesn't sting and it doesn't burn, it just weighs all around you like some sick, nauseous gravity, that's what you did to me, OK? The day I called your house and your father told me you'd left town for college? Excuse me? And not to call back . . . are you kidding? Seventeen years old and this adult who knows his son has made me pregnant says, "Don't call back"? Do you have any idea how alone I felt? God, I felt so alone! And now you show up here twenty years later, talking about old times . . . and you think you can ask me out for some kind of weird penitential date at the Shoreview without even really mentioning what you've done . . . like it'll be in bad taste or something even to bring it up, and I'm willing to sit here and *listen*? That's so *sick*.

PETER: But that's exactly what I want to talk about, if you'd just give me a chance—

KARI: No! I never had a chance from the day we met, and now you don't get one either! Every molecule of my life is, like . . . seventeen degrees off from where it should have been . . . and it all started with you. Because of you, I'm seventeen degrees and an eternity away from everything under the sun, and my baby—instead of a baby, I have a shadow of a baby, and it stretches across my whole . . . goddamned . . . life.

PETER: I do, too!

KARI: No, you don't, you have nothing but a giant sucking need!

PETER: Kari, I didn't make you get rid of that baby!

KARI: So what was I supposed to do?

PETER: You could have kept it!

KARI: And you could have stayed!

PETER: I know! And I wish that I had! I wish I had fought harder to do what was right, I wish I had spent the past twenty years with you and our baby instead of alone as the world's greatest fuck-up, I wish I could go back in time and do it all over again—

KARI: And what, you want some kind of fucking credit for wishing? Wishing is nothing! It's just like "sorry," it's nothing and it refers to nothing! God. Everything since the beginning of time was working together to make my happiness possible; and then you, you walked into the audiovisual lab in your flannel shirt . . . and you fucked it up! You fucked everything up! Do you understand that? Because of you, the entire universe is ruined . . . forever!

[*Brief pause.*]

NARRATOR [*as* NARRATOR, *to the audience*]: We'll take a short break.

[*Music rises. Lights down.*]

ACT 2

[*The scene is the dock that extends from the doors of the Pavilion and out to the edge of the lake. Light rises on the* NARRATOR.]

NARRATOR [*to the audience*]: In the middle of life, we find ourselves alive. Disoriented; lost; but alive. Time, like an immense pavilion, stretches above us, behind us, and ahead of us—sand beneath our feet—how did we get here? We can remember one moment ago with what seems at first to be an intense accuracy: we were standing right there; we were saying *thus* and *thus;* a decision was made, irreversible effects were somehow caused by the causes of other effects, we swear we were standing right there . . . but already it blurs and decays, and the wind in our faces, all the oncoming moments wash over us with a deafening roar, we're pulled forward, and then back, by memory's undertow, forward and back . . . it's dizzying. And does the future exist? Is it already there, an undiscovered landscape, waiting in shadow just beyond our footfall, down we go, there it is, ahhhh; or do we stand at a precipice, eternally falling onto a track on which only a runaway train can lie? Do we become by forgetting or by remembering the past? Are we building ourselves, or are we rather foaming into existence on the developing curve of a wave? At the edge of the water, at the edge of the land, on the shore of the past and the future we stand; somehow, in the middle of life, as if born again in the foam of the ancient oceans, we wake in the wake and we find ourselves: alive.

[KARI *enters, with a champagne bottle and glass. She sits on the edge of the stage.*]

It's ten o'clock. Outside the Pavilion, here in the dark beyond the beach and the volleyball nets, a few couples are preparing to leave early, to pick up the kids at Grandma's, to start the long drive home to Breckenridge, Moorhead, or Devil's Lake. Inside, the pounding darkness is lit intermittently by a sudden strobe light, a flash, revealing all at once a dance floor packed with bodies and a windowsill that stretches for one hundred and five feet along the southern wall, lined with beer glasses, wine coolers, napkins, and an undone tie. And a few pairs of high-school sweethearts are sitting cross-legged out on the dock, talking about old times, and tenderly brushing the occasional mosquito away from a longed-for cheek. Far above the earth, the stars are slowly wheeling around Polaris . . .

[PETER *enters, carrying his guitar in its case.*]

PETER: I'm leaving.
KARI: Good-bye.
NARRATOR [*to the* TECH, *in a bit of a rush*]: Could we have some stars please?

[*Scant stars come out.*]

PETER: Angie told me you were out here. I thought you went home.
KARI: Right, like I'm in a hurry to go home.
NARRATOR: Would it be asking too much to actually have the northern hemisphere near the summer solstice in the year 2005? Quickly?

[*The sky fills up with stars.*]

PETER: Anyway . . . I've got a long drive back, so . . .

[*The* NARRATOR *traces a path across the sky and a shooting star races by.*]

KARI: Oh, Peter, look!
NARRATOR [*to the* TECHS]: Thank you.
PETER: What?
KARI: Didn't you see that?
PETER: No, what was it?
KARI: I don't know, a shooting star, maybe? Or a comet? What is the difference, anyway, between a shooting star and a comet?
PETER: I don't know, I never really listened in science.
KARI: Me neither.

[*Brief pause.*]

Just stick around a second, maybe it'll happen again.
PETER [*surprised at the invitation*]: OK.
NARRATOR [*to the audience*]: In human history, every little thing makes a difference.

[PETER *sits down cautiously, not too close to* KARI. *There should be ample space left for silence and contemplation of the stars in between lines in the scene that follows.*]

KARI: How long until midnight?
PETER: I don't know, I don't wear a watch.
KARI: Me neither. Can you tell time by the stars?

[*They both look up.*]

PETER: Not really. It must not be midnight yet, though, we're not on fire.

[*Brief pause.*]

KARI: I can't believe that dress Rhonda Porkonnen's wearing, can you?
PETER: I told her she looked like a big ripe strawberry.
KARI: You did? You dork.
PETER: No, she took it as a compliment, it kinda worked out. I got lucky.
KARI: I think her husband is a criminal.
PETER: The guy with the mustache?
KARI: Yeah, doesn't he just have that look?
PETER: He does have kind of a Snidely Whiplash thing going.
KARI: And I think I heard somewhere tonight that he was a . . . video pirate, or something. He pirates videos.

[*Beat.*]

PETER [*halfheartedly, like a pirate*]: *Aaarrrgh.*

[*Brief pause while they look at the stars.*]

KARI: I suppose you should get going. It doesn't look like anything else is gonna happen.
PETER: No, it doesn't, does it?

[*Beat.*]

Probably the minute I leave, though, there'll be some huge cosmic event, right, like fireworks in the sky and stuff.
KARI: Probably.
PETER: That's how my life usually works, anyway. I'm always missing things by just a few crucial minutes.
KARI: Seventeen degrees.
PETER: Yeah.
KARI: Me too.

[*Brief pause.*]

PETER [*with a sigh*]: Well . . . I guess . . .
KARI: You could stick around for a minute or two, maybe—
PETER [*jarred*]: Oh, sure . . . I could do that. No one's expecting me.
KARI: What about your girlfriend?
PETER [*totally taken aback*]: We don't live together, who told you I had a girlfriend?

KARI: I don't know, everyone in town who comes into the bank always feels compelled to tell me every little thing about you whenever they hear something.

PETER: You've known I've got a girlfriend all night?

KARI: Sure. Her name's Lou Ann or something?

PETER: Lou-Marie. But could we—

KARI [*rushing over his previous line*]: And she's a painter or something, right?

PETER: Yeah, but could we really not talk about this?

KARI: What does she paint?

PETER: Why didn't you say anything?

KARI: I was waiting to see if you'd bring her up, what does she paint? Tell me.

PETER: Still lifes.

KARI: Like fruit in a bowl and shit?

PETER: Yeah, like fruit in a bowl. And shit. But very realistic, it's not quite as dumb as it sounds. It's like you can reach out and touch everything she paints. Like her apples?—are very convincing.

KARI: That must be so great for you.

PETER: Look, I'm the one who said I didn't want to talk about her!

KARI: I know!

PETER: Don't pick on me when you're the one that asked—

KARI: And she's kinda young, isn't she?

PETER: Kari—

KARI: Isn't she?

PETER: I don't know . . . what is young nowadays?

KARI: How young is she? Someone else in town'll tell me if I really want to know. How young is she? Thirty?

PETER [*ashamed*]: Lower.

KARI: Twenty-eight?

PETER: Lower.

KARI: Twenty-seven?

PETER: Twenty-three.

KARI: *Twenty-three?!*

PETER: Yep.

KARI: Oh my God, Peter, what does she see in you?

PETER: I don't know, what did you see in me?

KARI: Somebody my own age! God!

PETER: I think—

KARI: This is astounding!

PETER: Thank you for saying that, I think what the deal is, is . . .

KARI: What?

PETER: I don't know. I think she's too young still to really get how fucked-up I am.

KARI: Oh, come on, she must know.

PETER: No, she doesn't.

KARI: Oh, she must.

PETER: Trust me, she doesn't.

KARI: So why didn't you bring her?

PETER: Why are you even talking to me?

[*The* NARRATOR *traces another shooting star across the sky.*]

KARI: Peter, look! Did you see that?

PETER: Yeah . . .

[*Beat.*]

KARI: So why didn't you bring her?

PETER: Oh Jesus, I don't know, Kari. I didn't bring her because . . . because I think we're kind of breaking up; or I'm kind of breaking up or something.

KARI: But you two have been together for like a while, right?

PETER: Three years.

KARI: So why are you breaking up with her, is she pregnant?

PETER [*taking the hit*]: No, it's just stopped being right.

KARI: Things with Hans and I stopped being right about ten years ago, Peter, we haven't let that keep us from wasting each other's lives, why are you breaking up with her? She's young, she paints fruit. Is there somebody else?

PETER: Kinda.

KARI: What does that mean? You just have your eye on somebody? Who is she?

[*Brief pause.*]

PETER: Could I maybe have a little, umm . . . champagne?

KARI: Oh, sure.

[*She pours him a glass.*]

One of the little perks of being on the food committee. Knowing where they hide the champagne.

PETER: Where is it?

KARI: Like I'd tell you.

[*Brief pause, while they drink.*]

It's under the stage. So who is she?

PETER: You.

[*Brief pause.*]

KARI: God . . .

PETER: What?

KARI: I'm gonna go.

[*She rises.*]

PETER: Don't! Forget I said it!

KARI: How can I? God! Peter, you are such a mess, do you know that?

PETER: I know, I'm a mess because I'm not with you!

KARI: No, you're a mess, period! Look at yourself! You're thirty-seven years old, you're here with that stupid guitar, and you're telling me these things and I'm married! God, I swear, you are the only person I know who works in the field of mental health and you are the most screwed-up person I know! I mean, tell me something, that song you sang tonight, the one you wrote—

PETER: You didn't like it?

KARI: No, it's not that, how can you write such a beautiful song—this is such a mystery to me—how can you write a beautiful song like that . . . and still be so stupid about everything, to think you could come back and say something like that?

PETER: Everybody's stupid about everything!

KARI: Oh, is that what you tell people down in the Cities? Is that what they pay you to tell them, everybody's fucked-up and don't worry about it?

PETER: Well, aren't they? Deep down? About what matters?

KARI: Not everybody! A lot of people have it together!

PETER: Who? Are you at the same party I'm at? Who here tonight has their shit together? Who? Really?

KARI: Denise Charbonneau.

PETER: How could she? Her father was murdered when she was six.

KARI: Oh yeah—

PETER: Remember, she got that special award at graduation for being such a survivor?

KARI: I totally spaced it out—

PETER: She's never had a steady relationship in her life, she obviously hasn't come to terms with her sexual orientation—

KARI: You don't think so?

PETER: No—

KARI: I don't think so either—

PETER: —she drinks like a fish, and in the meantime, she spends her time traveling the globe, stamping out drugs!? You saw her going after Cookie tonight, I thought she was going to arrest him, what kind of life is that?

KARI: It's a life, don't judge!

PETER: I know, but is this a woman with her shit together?

KARI: Denny and Sonya have their shit together!

PETER: Kari, Denny has been sleeping with Tina Hawkenson ever since grade school!

KARI: How do you know that?

PETER: He told me tonight! The way Denny sees it, he's cheating on Tina by being married to Sonya, not the other way around! And he's really torn up about it, he had me in the corner for twenty minutes pouring his heart out—

KARI: That doesn't make any sense—

PETER: Sure it does, I feel that way about you with everybody.

KARI: OK, I got it!

PETER: What?

KARI: I know who has their shit together.

PETER: Who?

KARI: Me.

PETER: You've got your shit together.

KARI: I do. In my way. I go to work every day, I go home, I go to work, I do my thing, I don't complain.

PETER: And you're happy with Hans.

KARI: That's not the point! The point is, I don't complain! You know, everybody, Peter, they come down into the box where I work, and they complain, they tell me their troubles, you know? For the past twenty years, I've been listening to people complain. It's a lot like your job, I bet, except at your office the secrets are in the people's heads, and where I work, they keep them in boxes, but the dynamic's the same, "blah blah blah blah blah!" They come down there when they're getting divorced, or when somebody dies, or when they just want to see their stuff, you know, when they feel a little nervous about their valuables, and there I am, right, I must not have anything to do or say, I'm just Kari, I've been there forever, I'll be there forever, so they come down there and they open their boxes and "blah blah blah blah blah!" But see, I don't put other people through that, I don't complain, I don't even open my box, I just leave it all in there where it's safe and I shut up and do my job, you know? I don't make everybody else pay for my problems, they're mine! And maybe, according to you, that's not having your shit together, but as far as I'm concerned, given how fucked-up the universe is, it'll do!

PETER: But you're not happy!

KARI: Nobody's happy like they thought they'd be!

PETER: So you don't even think happiness is possible?

KARI: Like you mean it, probably, no.

PETER: How do you think I mean it?

KARI: Like "la dee dah dee tra la la!"

PETER: But see, that's not what I mean, I just mean that it's exciting and—

KARI: Bearable?

PETER: No, better than bearable!

KARI: How could it be, Peter, it's life! Bearable's the best we can hope for!

PETER: See, I can't believe that! I won't!

KARI: Really, this morning, Hans was *inside* me, right?

[PETER *smiles tightly, not really ready*—]

Just listen, he was inside my *body*. If there's anybody else on earth I can tell this to, it's you. I get one life, right, and one body, and this morning Hans was inside it. And we were all finished, but he was still on top of me and I could tell he was thinking about something. So I said, like a dope, "What are you thinking about?" And he said, "A really difficult hole." And it wasn't even a joke. That's what I live with. Me and that, alone every night in a split-level pro shop with beds for the human beings to rest on in between rounds! On a good day, it's bearable. On a bad day, you don't know.

PETER: What?

KARI: He's *so* mad, Peter. In his mind, he rescued me from the jaws of ill repute, right, because you'd dumped me and I'd had an abortion and "oh God," right, and he brought me out to be the Baroness Von Nine Iron of the most beautiful executive golf course in Becker County! And he *did* rescue me, kind of, see, that's the real problem, he did! And he was really sweet about it too, I mean, I can see his point, because I had been really lonely ever since you broke up with me, and Hans was so chivalrous about it, he took me out around town like it was all perfectly normal even though everybody always looked at us funny. One time he took me to the Voyager and he announced to the whole bar that we were getting married and he bought everyone a round of drinks. And Arne Neubeck was really drunk, like he always is, and he came over and said to Hans, "You just made the biggest fucking mistake of your life." And Hans punched him so fast and so hard, he knocked the wind out of that entire room, and I got a dozen roses the next day from Arne with an apology. So Hans was really sweet, and he rescued me, and all he ever wanted from me in return, the way he sees it, all he ever wanted from me was a "motherfucking baby" . . . and I wouldn't give him one, and *I won't give him one,* and his parents are all pissed off at me about it, but he's too nice to leave me and I can't change, it's just . . . *bad*! It's such an *awful, bad home.*

[*Very long pause.*]

PETER: Hey.

KARI: What?

PETER: Listen. You get this much time in your one life, right?

KARI: Yeah?

PETER: Like you said, with your body, only this much. And you get this many people. Only this many. And out of the time and the people you're given you make what you make, and that's your life, right?

KARI: Right . . .

PETER: But what if there's such a thing as destiny, do you ever think about that?

KARI: There isn't.

PETER: But what if there is in the sense that, what if there was a person who could unlock the key to your life precisely because of what you did to them or what they did to you, or because you were stupid like me and you just missed it the first time around? Destiny like that, nothing cosmic. What if . . . what if it's like life, where when you're young you think it's gonna be about a lot of things and you prepare yourself for it, thinking, "Life is gonna be so wild, there's gonna be so much coming at me from every direction, how will I ever keep up?" That's what I always thought, and let me tell you, I sat down all ready to get my hair blown back by this explosion of millions of experiences that never ever came. And so the question becomes, what if you open your eyes after that and there's suddenly just one person, and it turns out that in some sense your entire life is really all about what you're gonna do about this one person and then what if you made a mistake? Are you telling me there's only one chance?

KARI: Doesn't it seem that way?

PETER: The whole world exists so that everyone gets just one chance?

KARI: Yes!

PETER: One chance is enough of a reason to make a whole world? You're telling me there's no mercy, there's no forgiveness, there's no air in the system to breathe and no room to move and we're just trapped in the net of what we've done forever? Look, I was young and I was scared and I made a mistake. A big mistake. And I know it hasn't cost me what it cost you to live without that baby, but it's cost me a lot. It has. But when I look at you now, Kari, and I see those little wrinkles around your eyes . . . ? And I realize I've missed so much of you already . . . ? The thought that I won't see the rest, that I won't get to know you any better and hold your hand and see you smile . . . and then one day you'll be gone forever? That breaks my heart.

KARI: Peter . . .

PETER: I can't live any further into my life without *you*. Please. Come back to the Cities with me tonight. Get a divorce. Marry me. Or live with me. Or let's have another baby and just be friends, I don't care, let's . . . just . . . come on. We'll start over.

KARI: Peter, we can't.

PETER: Look, whatever we've done, both our lives are a mess, right? A mess! And I've got a car and a full tank of gas.

[*Beat.*]

Are you coming?

KARI [*amused at his bravado*]: Who do you think you are?

PETER: I am the guy who sang "Mandy" in swing choir. I am the guy who played Lancelot in *Camelot*. I am one half of the Cutest Senior Couple and I'm leaving and I want you to come with me! Come on!

KARI: No!

PETER: Why, because you'd rather stay married to Hans, who hates you? In this town where they burn things down that oughta last forever? Or is it that you'd rather have me feel lousy forever than be happy for one more minute yourself?

KARI: Do you ever think about anything but you?

PETER: Yes, I'm offering you a way out!

KARI: To YOU! I need a way to ME!

PETER: Can't I be a way to you? You're a way to me?

KARI: Not everybody sees people like that, Peter! Just you!

PETER: All I want is a chance to start over!

KARI: Peter, for you and me to start over, the entire universe would have to begin again.

[*Brief pause.*]

What?

PETER: Say that again.

KARI: For you and me to start over, the whole universe would have to begin again.

[*Long pause.* PETER *turns and glances at the* NARRATOR, *who looks away.* PETER *looks back at* KARI, *who is quietly living with the simple sadness of the impossibility. And then* PETER *gets up—*]

KARI: Where are you going?

PETER: Hang on a second.

[*He goes to the* NARRATOR *and stands by him for a moment.*]

PETER [*to the* NARRATOR]: Hi.

NARRATOR [*gracious but taken aback*]: Hello.

PETER: Listen, can you start the entire universe all over again?

NARRATOR: No.

PETER: No, come on, sure you can, you just say . . . "This is the way the universe begins" and all that other hocusy-pocusy shit, right?

NARRATOR: No.

PETER: You *can* do it, right, you just *won't.*

NARRATOR: What exactly would be the difference? To you?

PETER: Come on—just this once—

NARRATOR: It's not possible.

PETER: Because you won't *let* it be.

NARRATOR: No, because it's simply not. I could start another universe, if you like, a different one . . . with a different voice and different words, but not this one again. Not these stars, not this world, not this Pavilion.

PETER: Would she and I be in the new universe if you did that?

NARRATOR: No.

PETER: Then what would be the point?

NARRATOR: Exactly. Don't you see, I don't make the rules? I'm working within limits just like you, I'm not in charge.

PETER: Bullshit.

NARRATOR: It's true. Time only goes in one direction, that's your problem. It's not you, it's not her, it's time. I'm sorry.

PETER: No, don't apologize, that's great—

NARRATOR: It's just, you're asking the wrong person for the wrong thing. I could try something else if you wanted—

PETER: No! That's fine! Fuck it! I don't need you! I'll do it myself! Let's see.

[*Brief pause.*]

[*To the audience*] This is the way the universe begins, a raindrop drops, uhh, now but backwards, boom, sloop, up, it's a little pavilion—

NARRATOR [*to the audience*]: Just so everyone's clear—the universe isn't actually starting over.

PETER: Water, continents, insects, creatures—

NARRATOR: Time only goes in one direction . . .

PETER: —the tea leaf of consciousness, the primitive mind—

NARRATOR: . . . and this is just a desperate ploy.

PETER: —love, morality, whoosh, it's a little pavilion! Europe, time, the Renaissance, time, the steam engine, my family, me—

NARRATOR: Look away! I mean it, look away! It's bad magic!

PETER: Uhh, oh, umm, my great-grandmother wrote a book, it's called *Pioneer Days*, it's in the Library of Congress, there's a house on the hill on the shore of the lake—that's you—this is the Pavilion and this is a play about time!

[*Brief pause. And then, remembering what he'd somehow forgot . . .*]

This is a play about time.

[*Long pause.*]

[*To the* NARRATOR] That didn't change a thing, did it?

NARRATOR: No.

PETER [*to* KARI]: You're still married to Hans?

KARI: Yeah.

PETER: And I'm still me.

[*Very long pause. Finally,* KARI *speaks. Simply. Not sympathetically. This is about her.*]

KARI: It's OK.

[*A long beat.*]

I don't want the universe to start over.

PETER: You don't?

KARI: No, I don't.

[*Beat.*]

[*Very gently*] Do you remember that day in the spring of junior year . . . ? It was really hot . . . and you came and got me out of study hall and we skipped out and went to the Sandwich Hut for a crunch cone? And we walked down here by the lake, and I told you I was hot, and you *picked me up*. Do you remember that?

PETER: Yeah.

KARI: You picked me up *just like in a movie* and you kinda dipped me back into the water so I could get my hair wet. And when you did that . . . I saw the sunshine upside down making . . . glittering little bubbly patterns on the water, like I was on a Ferris wheel, kind of, and, boom! it was like all the feelings in the lower parts of my body swooshed back up into my head, and as you lifted me up out of the water, I tilted up and all my thoughts, swoosh, all my sensibility rushed down into my underwear and I looked at you and you looked so handsome, Peter, I just suddenly knew it was the right time. And I felt so silly because just like ten minutes before I had said all that stuff to you about how I was always going to be a virgin, and I *just* didn't see why people thought sex was *so* important. And we walked back to my house holding hands and your hand was shaking so hard. *God.*

[*Brief pause.*]

To be held like that, at that age; to see those shining things; and to walk that mile with you right down the middle of the street . . . I don't want to lose that. I don't want the universe to start over. I just want to let it *go*. I want to let it go *on*. OK?

NARRATOR [*to the audience, exactly as at the beginning, without special emphasis*]: This is the way the universe begins.

KARI [*to* PETER]: OK?

[PETER *lives with the pain of* KARI's *words for a long moment.*]

NARRATOR [*to the audience*]: At every single moment, the whole creation is beginning again, stretching the tent of the present moment to bursting. And the waves that push up through the oceans, and the waves that push up through the stars; and the waves that push upwards through history are the same waves that push up through us. And so we *have to say yes to time,* even though it means speeding forward into memory; forgetfulness; and oblivion. Say no to time; hold on to what you were or what she was; hold on to the past, even out of love . . . and I swear it will tear you to shreds. This universe will tear you to shreds.

[*Brief pause.*]

PETER: Kari, I am so sorry that, uh, we only get one life, and that I wasn't better to you.

KARI: I know.

[*Long pause.*]

PETER: The day you told me you were pregnant, I went home and told my dad, and he was, like, "Son, here's what we're gonna do," and I knew it wasn't right; I knew that he had married my mom when she got pregnant and he had always been mad about it, and he wanted me to . . . it doesn't matter what he wanted, I just knew it wasn't right, but I did it. And I'm sorry.

KARI: I know.

PETER: But I want you to know, I feel really lucky that I got the chance to know you, and to see the way you are as a person. And I just hope that maybe someday, after we die or something, who knows, you know, maybe we could . . .

[*Beat.*]

KARI: . . . hang out?

PETER: Yeah, maybe we could hang out and . . . just remember how it was.

KARI: I don't really think we'll be able to remember anything.

PETER: I'm going to. I'm gonna remember everything.

[*The* NARRATOR *abruptly enters the scene as* KENT.]

NARRATOR [*as* KENT]: Hey, you guys.

KARI: Hi, Kent.

NARRATOR: I'm sorry, you guys, but you gotta clear outta here. The fire department wants to start setting up the pumps on the lake.

KARI: Oh, so that's how they're gonna do it.

NARRATOR: Yeah. This is gonna be the biggest fire Pine City's ever seen. The trucks can't hold enough water. Besides, it gives the guys a chance to use the equipment. It's fun for 'em.

KARI: God, Kent, can you imagine the Pavilion not being here?

NARRATOR: No.

KARI: And some big ugly concrete thing?

NARRATOR: I know. I didn't vote for it. Cookie said he'd get me Hank Williams Jr.'s autograph if I'd get behind it, but what do I care about that? This is where everything happens that matters.

KARI: Kent, did you ever ... find Cookie?

NARRATOR: Yeah. He's funny.

PETER: Yeah, he is.

NARRATOR: I've never been funny.

[*Beat.*]

KARI: You didn't ... kill him, did you?

NARRATOR: No ... I didn't ... I didn't do anything. I saw him and I ... didn't do anything. You guys—

KARI: What?

NARRATOR: I love Angie so much. I love her so much. But I've wasted so much time, I mean, shit, this is our twenty-year reunion! Twenty years I've been with her, but where have I been really, I don't know! And how much time is left, I mean, you know what I mean? I'm not making much sense, probably. Cookie got me high.

KARI: Kent, you're the chief of police!

NARRATOR: I know I am!

KARI: And you got high?

NARRATOR: What can I say, it's complicated. It's all complicated. When I woke up this morning, I thought there was a God, I thought there was justice, I thought there was a right way to live. And now, all I know for sure is I haven't loved Angie as much as I wanted to when we were young and now that's all a mess and time's running out and I look up at the stars and I don't see anything but ... stars.

[*Long pause.*]

PETER: They're kinda beautiful anyway, though, huh?

NARRATOR [*still disappointed*]: Yeah, they'll do.

[*Long pause.*]

I'll settle for stars.

[*Brief pause.*]

KARI [*to* KENT]: Hey, Kent, can *you* tell time by the stars?

NARRATOR: Actually, Kari ... Hari-Kari ... I bet no one's called you that for a while ... I can. [*To the audience, as* NARRATOR] It's twelve o'clock.

[*Lights shift. Glitter ball starts. Music begins.*]

    [*To* TECHS] Thank you. [*To the audience*]
And that means it's time for the sweetheart dance, everybody

    So find that old flame and give it one last go, and then we'll burn the place down

    Good-bye!

    If you want some pot, later, I can get you some, all you want

    There's a chance we won't ever see each other again

    I tried taking in a day-care kid, but you know, this is going to sound unkind—I didn't like him

    This is my wife, Karen; Karen, this is Andrea

    And they've already created photons in the lab that can surpass the speed of light

    They look cute together

[PETER *and* KARI *come together to dance.*]

    but you don't like being at home with your kids?—see, that's such a shame, because I would give anything to be able to stay at home with our kids

    It's gonna be two hours to get TO the airport, and then two hours to get THROUGH the airport, so, yeah

    We should go

    Of course I still love you; but God forgives me for that, don't you think?

    You dip three fingers into the Sambuca and then you light them on fire— ouch!—while you shoot the rest

Yes, that would mean time stands still for the person on the ship but not for the observer

Hold me tighter

I read somewhere that repentance is being in the same situation later and not doing it

I've tried it twice, just can't get it started

And what if we were living during the long, slow end of the world, or a paradigm shift, or an axial age?

I'm thinking of starting my own business

I saw the way you looked at him

Because I'm sick of teaching piano

Either way, how can there not be a tremendous collapse on the horizon?

And these are our three little boys

If I could just get my act together, I'd go back to school, and get a master's or a doctorate

Something I can believe in, you know?

God, I don't believe in anything sometimes I look up and wonder if anybody's really watching

We should probably go back in, it's the last dance, people will start to wonder

It's different, we have fun, we go out

No, it's not what it *was*, what I *thought* it would be, but it's good

Don't let me go, please, don't ever let me go

And the great thing is we have deer in the yard on a regular basis!

We're planning on moving

Yeah, getting out

Someday

Hold me

Maybe someday

Yeah, I'm still waiting tables, but the money's great and I have lots of spare time

Oh, I'm just glad to be a happy survivor of the good old days, you know?

I'm singing in a band, and painting, you know, in my spare time

God

Spare time

Like, who will ever remember what it was like, you know, when we're gone?

I'm divorced
Staying up at the cabin

I'm divorced

Just two little kitties named Sadie and Sylvia

[PETER *and* KARI *separate.* KARI *exits.*]

And who will ever remember I loved her that way, or the way she looked that day?

I see him with her now, I can't take it

Bow-hunting, golfing, fishing, you know, jack-of-all trades, master of none

The children keep us pretty busy, but we'll have plenty of time for ourselves in four more years

Five more years

Oh, maybe ten more years

No, I know exactly what you mean, because sometimes I swear I can almost feel myself being remembered

And the fact that we'll all be gone and not a trace left behind

I meant to do more with my life, you know?

Hurry up!

There are so many things we don't say

I wish you could stay

I wish we could too

Good-bye!

[PETER *exits.*]

Good-bye!

Good-bye!

Good-bye!

Of course my heart's broken but all in all I'm very happy because life's been good.

APPENDIX

Down in the Ruined World

Lyrics by Craig Wright

Music by Peter Lawton
and Craig Wright

Down in the Ruined World, p. 2

Down in the Ruined World, p. 3